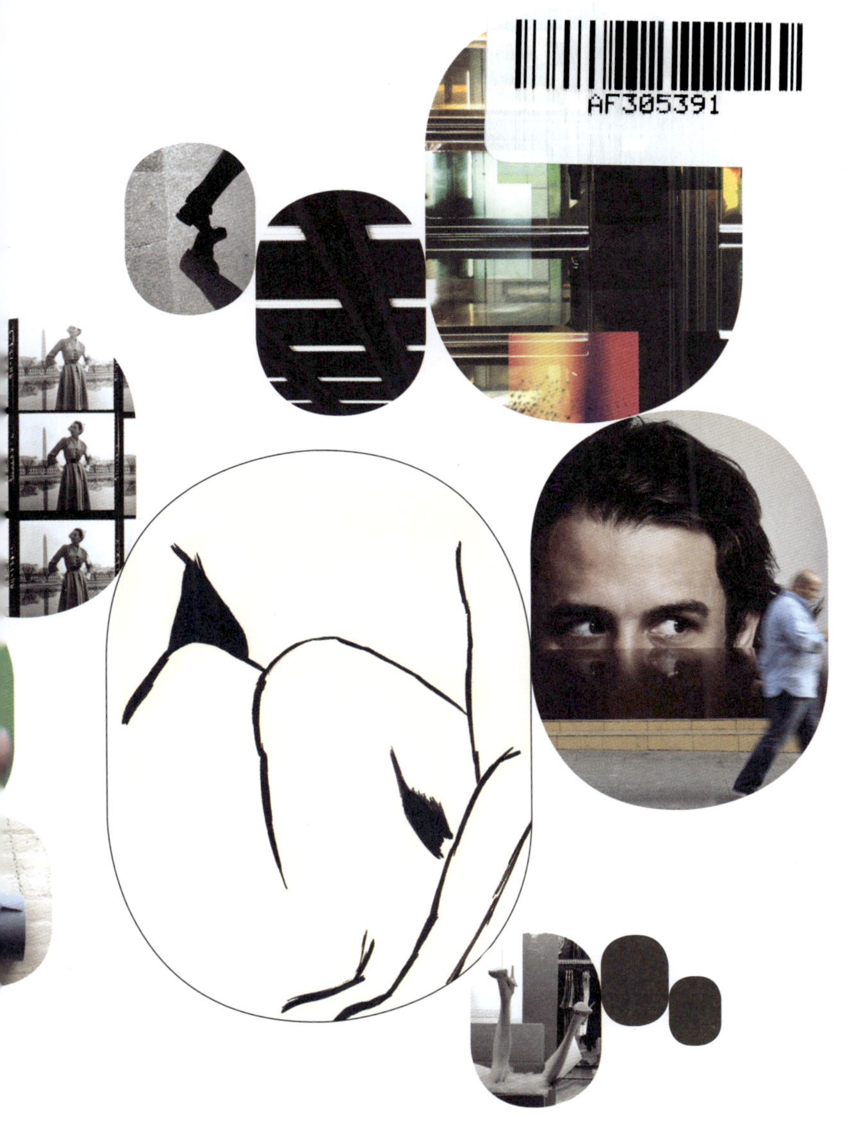
AF305391

Never
Photograph
People
Eating

And 50 other
Ridiculous Photography Rules

COLOPHON

BIS Publishers
Het Sieraad
Postjesweg 1
1057 DT Amsterdam
The Netherlands
T (+) 31 (0)20-515 02 30
F (+) 31 (0)20-515 02 39
bis@bispublishers.nl
www.bispublishers.nl

ISBN 978-90-6369-277-3

Copyright © 2013 BIS Publishers
Second printing 2013

Ridiculous Design Rules is a concept developed
by Lemon Scented Tea and commissioned by
Premsela, Dutch Platform for Design and Fashion
(www.premsela.org).

Editorial Director: Anneloes van Gaalen
(www.paperdollwriting.com)
Designed by: Lilian van Dongen Torman
(www.lilianvandongentorman.com)
Proofreading: Sarina Ruiter-Bouwhuis

BIS PUBLISHERS

Never Photograph People Eating

And 50 other
Ridiculous Photography Rules

CONTENTS

INTRODUCTION

Photography is more popular – and indeed more affordable – than ever. Reasonably-priced DSRL cameras, cheap photography apps and photo sharing sites, such as Instagram and Flickr, have all helped to bring the art of photography to a much wider, and ever-expanding, public. But as we all know: a good camera doesn't necessarily make for a good photographer. High time to share some photography guidelines, as well as some do's and don'ts.

The rules that govern the world of photography range from the reasonable – "Freeze the Action" – to the ridiculous – "Never Photograph People Eating." This book contains 51 photography rules that will hopefully appeal to both the professional photographer, as well as the enthusiastic amateur.

Rules such as "Frame Your Image," "Crop Well" and "The Rule of Thirds." Rules that to some are valuable words of wisdom, while others perceive them as ridiculous guidelines that need to be bended, twisted or broken altogether.

Never Photograph People Eating and 50 Other Ridiculous Photography Rules is the seventh book in a series that focuses on rules that people working in the creative industry – graphic designers, fashion designers, typographers, advertisers and filmmakers – can rely on, or ignore altogether. Future publications include *Never Touch A Painting When It's Wet And 50 other Ridiculous Art Rules*.

Don't touch the models

The relationship between the photographer and the model is one that is based on trust. As a photographer you need to trust your model to be able to take directions and bring his or her A-game. The chances of that happening are greatly increased when you remember to handle your model with care. Explain your plans, be respectful in your directions, show them what you've shot and never ever touch them without their permission.

———————

"A model can only be successfully directed by talking her into a mood or attitude. The moment you physically place a limb into position you may as well be photographing a shop dummy."
Sam Haskins (1926-2009), British photographer

"The model has to give you the moment. It's not you making it. They give it to you and you capture it."
Peter Lindberg (1944), German photographer

"The art of posing the photograph
is different from that of taking things
as they are. I think my best pictures
are not a result of a 'decisive moment,'
they are done in a 'moment of trust.'
No picture of mine was staged or
posed by myself. Sometimes people
spontaneously posed for me and
I simply took the picture, which they
offered. "
*Markéta Luskačová (1944), Czech
photographer*

"There are good reasons for using
oneself as a model (…) of course:
your model is the most intriguing and
puzzling person in the whole world;
(…) you're always available; you're
cheap; no explanations are needed
(...); you don't have to keep the model
happy; and the model gets tired, and
wants to stop, at exactly the same
moment as you do."
*Julian Flynn (1964), British
photographer*

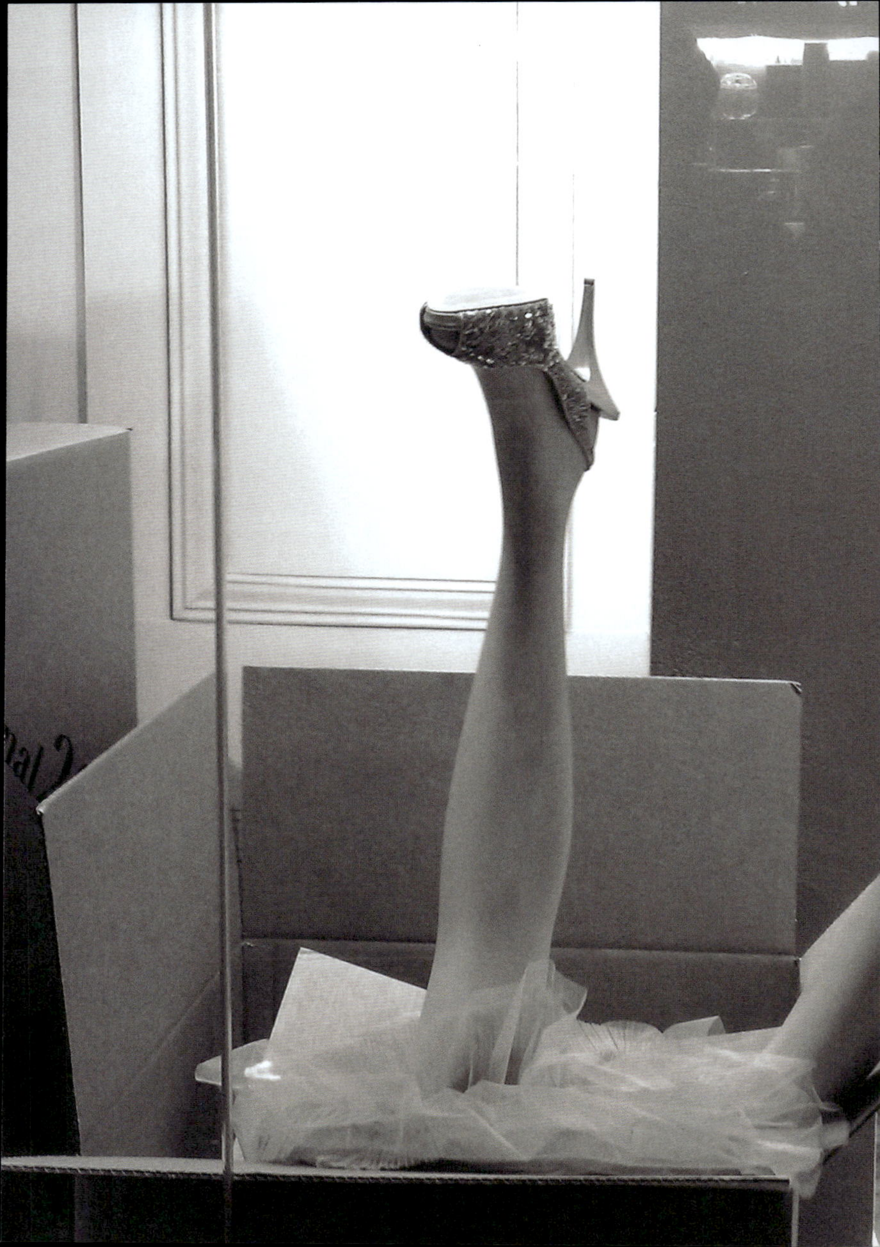

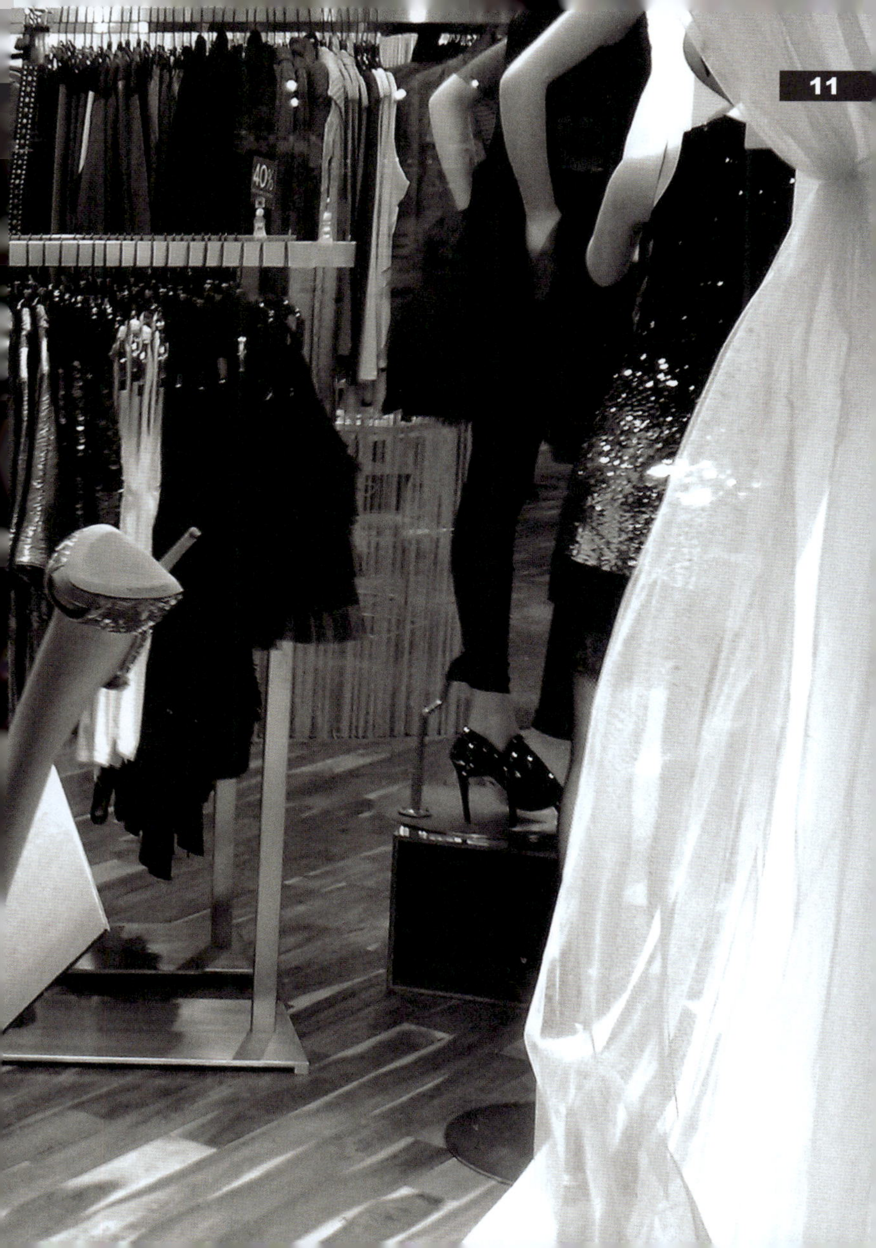

Photography is a game of chance

Instead of fighting the weather conditions when shooting outdoors or desperately dealing with setbacks in a studio environment, seasoned photographers know they can't control everything and that they're forever chasing an image that is fleeting. Accept the sobering reality that photography is to some extent a game of chance: it will make your photographic endeavors so much more enjoyable or at the very least less frustrating.

"The vital elements are often momentary, change-sent things... a gleam of light on water, a trail of smoke from a passing train, a cat crossing the threshold. Sometimes they are a matter of luck, sometimes of patience, waiting for an effect to be repeated that you have seen. It is usually some incidental detail that heightens the effect of a picture, stressing a pattern, deepening the sense of atmosphere."
Bill Brandt (1904-1983), British photographer

"Chance is always there. We all use it. The difference is, a poor photographer meets chance one out of a hundred times and a good photographer meets chance all the time."
George Brassaï (1899-1984), Hungarian photographer

"A lot depends on serendipity, making the most of the circumstances."
Julian Flynn (1964), British photographer

"When I start photographing, I never know how things will develop."
Viviane Sassen (1972), Dutch photographer

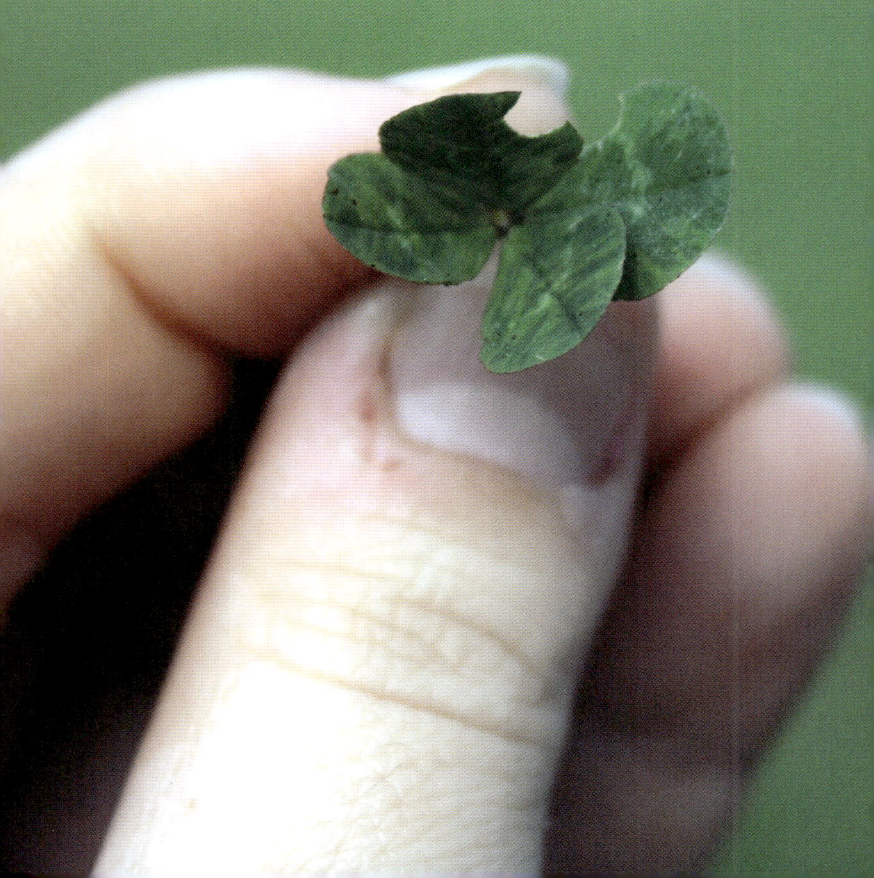

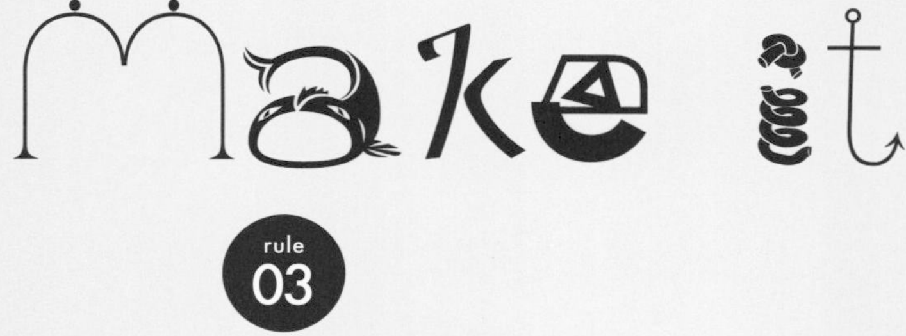

rule
03

Everybody knows that beauty is in the eye of the beholder. It's completely subjective, which makes any endeavor to create so-called 'pretty' pictures, whether or not to please a public, a ridiculous undertaking. Smarten up and take the following advice of American photographer Morley Baer (1916-1995) to heart: "Quit trying to find beautiful objects to photograph. Find the ordinary object so you can transform it by photographing it."

———————

"He who seeks beauty shall find it."
Bill Cunningham (1929), American photographer

"If you look at a photograph, and you think, 'My, isn't that a beautiful photograph,' and you go on to the next one, or 'Isn't that nice light?' so what? I mean what does it do to you or what's the real value in the long run? What do you walk away from it with? I mean, I'd much rather show you a photograph that makes demands on you, that you might become involved in on your own terms or be perplexed by."
Duane Michals (1932), American photographer

pretty

"The history of photography could be recapitulated as the struggle between two different imperatives: beautification... and truth-telling."
Susan Sontag (1933-2004), American writer and filmmaker

"I'm not into that approach to photography where everything has to be perfect; where every landscape has to be unspoiled; every flower has to be a perfect specimen, a drop of dew on each petal; every portrait showing the person at their best. I'm moved by the mess of life, the way we, and the world around us, falls short of our dreams and our ideals: but we still try to make something beautiful out of it anyway; and that beauty is more moving because it acknowledges our fallen state."
Julian Flynn (1964), British photographer

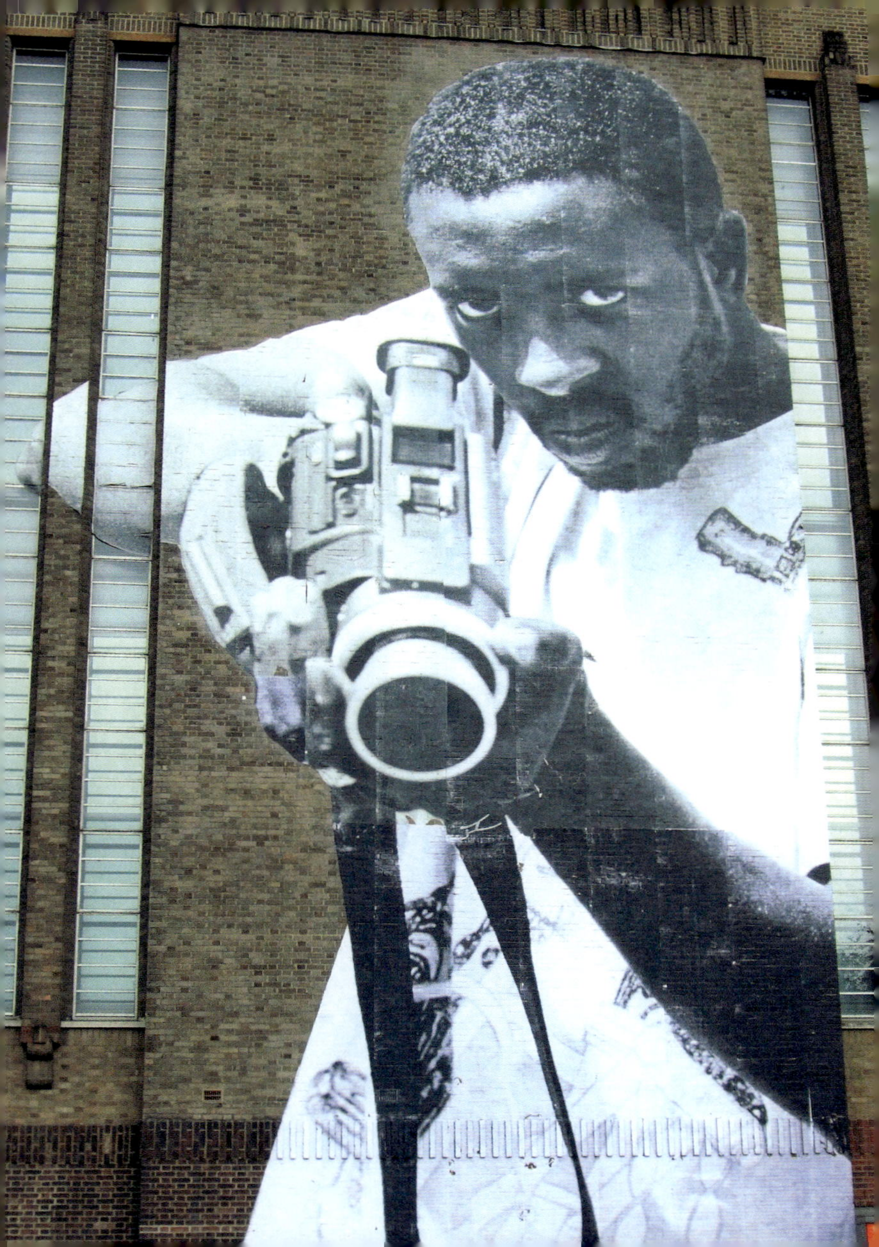

THE CAMERA IS A POWERFUL WEAPON

The pen is said to be mightier than the sword, but in an increasingly visual world the camera trumps them both.

———————

"Use photography as a weapon."
John Heartfield (1891-1968), German artist

"Photography has become a formidable weapon against truth in the hands of the bourgeoisie. The enormous quantity of picture material spit out daily by the printing press, that consequently appears to possess the character of truth, actually serves only to obscure the facts. The camera can lie just like the type-setting machine."
Bertolt Brecht (1898-1956), German poet and playwright

"Photography is a strong tool, a propaganda device, and a weapon for the defense of the environment... and therefore for the fostering of a healthy human race and even very likely for its survival."
Eliot Porter (1901-1990), American photographer

"You have a 45mm automatic pistol on your lap, and I have a 35mm camera on my lap, and my weapon is just as powerful as yours."
Gordon Parks (1912-2006), American photographer, writer and filmmaker to Black Panther militant Eldridge Cleaver

"The belief, the try, a camera and some film – the fragile weapons of my good intentions. With these I fought war."
W. Eugene Smith (1918-1978), American photographer

"We should remember that the power of photographs comes not only from their ability to copy reality, but also to alter reality. Photographs can be used – to borrow Heartfield's phrase – as weapons. They can be used to warn us about the dangers of impending war. They can also be used to ratchet up the blind forces of rage and unreason that drag us into conflict."
Errol Morris (1948), American director

"You don't take a photograph, you make it."

He is best known for his spectacular black-and-white photos of the American West. But Ansel Adams (1902-1984) contributed more to the world of photography than mere pictures. He authored a great number of books on the technical and theoretical aspects of photography. Known for spending hours upon hours creating the exact print of the picture he had envisioned, Adams firmly believed that "you don't take a photograph, you make it."

———————

"If you just click the shutter, you are stealing from reality! I can't be a thief! I must create!"
Barbara Morgan (1900-1992),
American photographer

"I never question what to do, it tells me what to do. The photographs make themselves with my help. "
Ruth Bernhard (1905-2006),
German-born American photographer

"A photograph is neither taken nor seized by force. It offers itself up. It is the photo that takes you. One must not take photos."
Henri Cartier-Bresson (1908-2004),
French photographer

"The pictures are there, and you just take them."
Robert Capa (1913-1954), Hungarian-born American photographer

"You don't take pictures; the good ones happen to you."
Ernst Haas (1921-1986), Austrian photographer

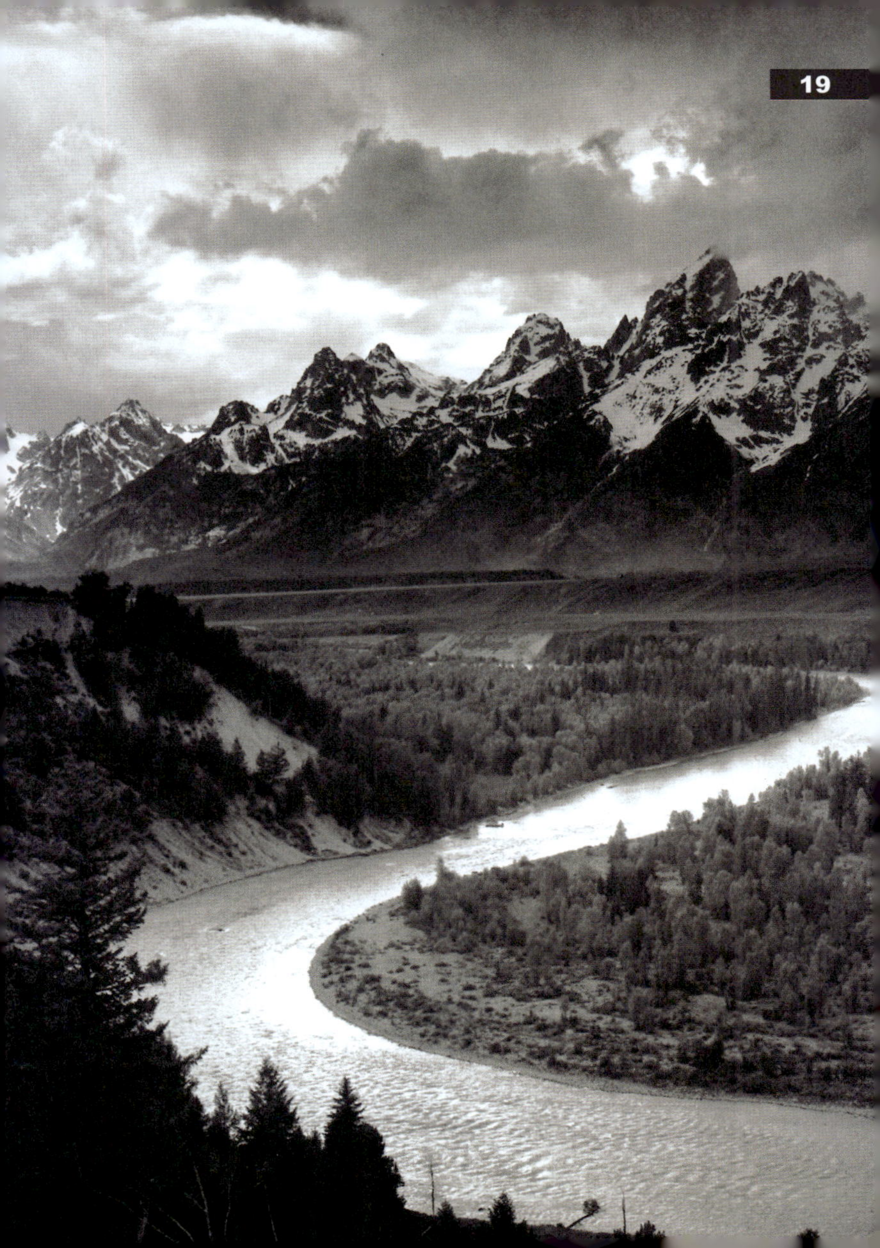

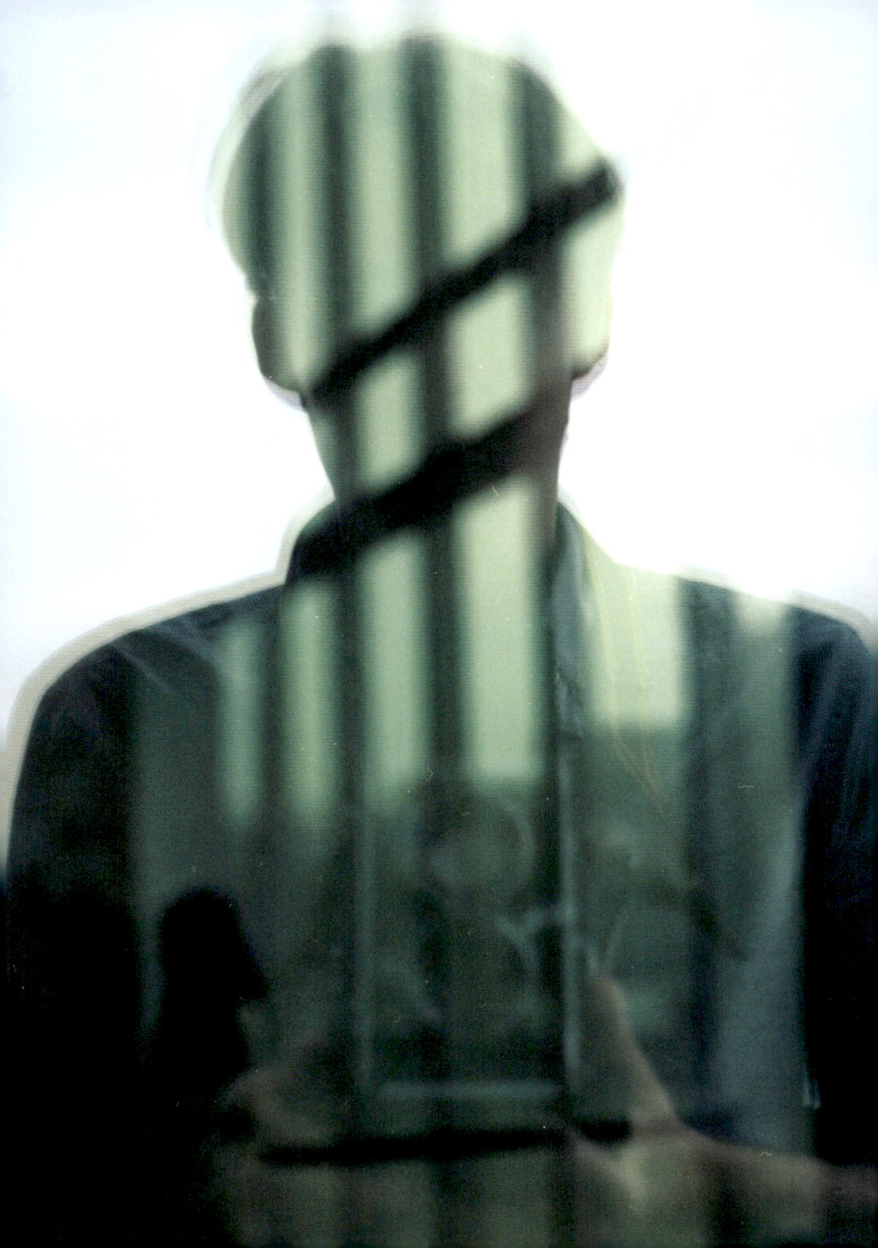

Shoot what you love

Shoot what you love. And shoot it often.

"Pick a theme and work it to exhaustion... the subject must be something you truly love or truly hate."
Dorothea Lange (1895-1965), American photographer

"Photograph things you really care about, things that really interest you, not things you feel you ought to do."
Chris Steele-Perkins (1947), British photographer

"No matter how much crap you gotta plow through to stay alive as a photographer, no matter how many bad assignments, bad days, bad clients, snotty subjects, obnoxious handlers, wigged-out art directors, technical disasters, failures of the mind, body, and will, all the shouldas, couldas, and wouldas that befuddle our brains and creep into our dreams, always remember to make room to shoot what you love. It's the only way to keep your heart beating as a photographer."
Joe McNally (1952), American photographer

"Find what you love, find what you want to say, find your style, and then go for it."
Ellen von Unwerth (1954), German photographer

Know your light

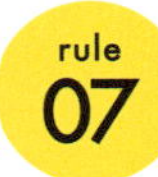

George Eastman (1854-1932), the American inventor and founder of Kodak Company, best described the intricate relationship between photography and light. He argued that "light makes photography," urging people to "Embrace light. Admire it. Love it. But above all, know light. Know it for all you are worth, and you will know the key to photography."

———————

"I have freed myself from the sticky medium of paint and am working directly with light itself."
Man Ray (1890-1976), American artist

"Light is my inspiration, my paint and brush. It is as vital as the model herself. Profoundly significant, it caresses the essential superlative curves and lines. Light I acknowledge as the energy upon which all life on this planet depends."
Ruth Bernhard (1905-2006), German-born American photographer

"It is light that reveals, light that obscures, light that communicates. It is light I 'listen' to. The light late in the day has a distinct quality, as it fades toward the darkness of evening. After sunset there is a gentle leaving of the light, the air begins to still, and a quiet descends. I see magic in the quiet light of dusk. I feel quiet, yet intense energy in the natural elements of our habitat. A sense of magic prevails. A sense of mystery. It is a time for contemplation, for listening – a time for making photographs."
John Sexton (1953), American photographer

"I don't work off lights and angles; I work off emotions. A mood that I create."
Terry Richardson (1965), American photographer

Keep Focus

Blurry photos might create an interesting artistic effect, but in general keeping focus makes for better photographs.

"You can't depend on your eyes if your imagination is out of focus."
Mark Twain (1835-1910),
American writer

"There is nothing worse than a sharp image of a fuzzy concept."
Ansel Adams (1902-1984),
American photographer

"Sharpness is a bourgeois concept."
Henri Cartier-Bresson (1908-2004),
French photographer

"My idea of a good picture is one that's in focus and of a famous person."
Andy Warhol (1928-1987), American
artist

"I like using snapshot cameras because they're idiot-proof. I have bad eyesight, and I'm no good at focusing big cameras."
Terry Richardson (1965), American
photographer

DON'T GET TOO INVOLVED

The rules that govern the field of photojournalism differ from those that photographers in other genres tend to adhere to. Photojournalists are reporters first and foremost and their job is to report on events, not intervene. In fact, in its Code of Ethics the National Press Photographers Association even calls on its members to "not intentionally contribute to, alter, or seek to alter or influence events" while photographing. Obviously, this is easier said than done and many a photojournalist has struggled with the desire to help or aid on the one hand and the need to simply observe and report on the other.

———

"In photojournalistic reporting, inevitably, you're an outsider."
Henri Cartier-Bresson (1908-2004), French photographer

"It's not always easy to stand aside and be unable to do anything except record the sufferings around one."
Robert Capa (1913-1954), Hungarian-born American photographer

"When you're working with a camera, you tend to disassociate yourself from what's going on. You're just an observer. We were there to record the facts. But there are moments when the facts are less important than somebody's life."
Ian Berry (1934), British photographer

"SEEING LOOKING AT WHAT OTHERS CANNOT BEAR TO SEE IS WHAT MY LIFE IS ALL ABOUT."

Don McCullin (1935), British photographer

"When I was taking other photographs for 'I Am Unbeatable', my book on domestic violence, I was there first as a photographer, not as a social worker. Yes, I would always be divided about whether to take a picture or defend the victim, but if I chose to put down my camera and stop one man from hitting one woman, I'd be helping just one woman. However, if I got the picture, I could help countless more."
Donna Ferrato (1949), American photographer

"For five years, I covered an awful lot of conflict – Baghdad, Afghanistan, all across Africa, the Middle East. The stuff that I saw there… On my first assignments in Iraq, I really struggled with it. It caused me so much stress, I got alopecia and lost all my hair all over my body. Just from thinking about all these things. The first time I experienced it, it actually stopped me taking images I really wanted to take or should have taken, because I was so mixed up and thinking: 'Should I be doing this or not?' I found it very difficult. But through experience, it's sad to say, you get immune to it. And then you can concentrate on your photography, and you feel that is your power."
Graeme Robertson (1978), British photographer

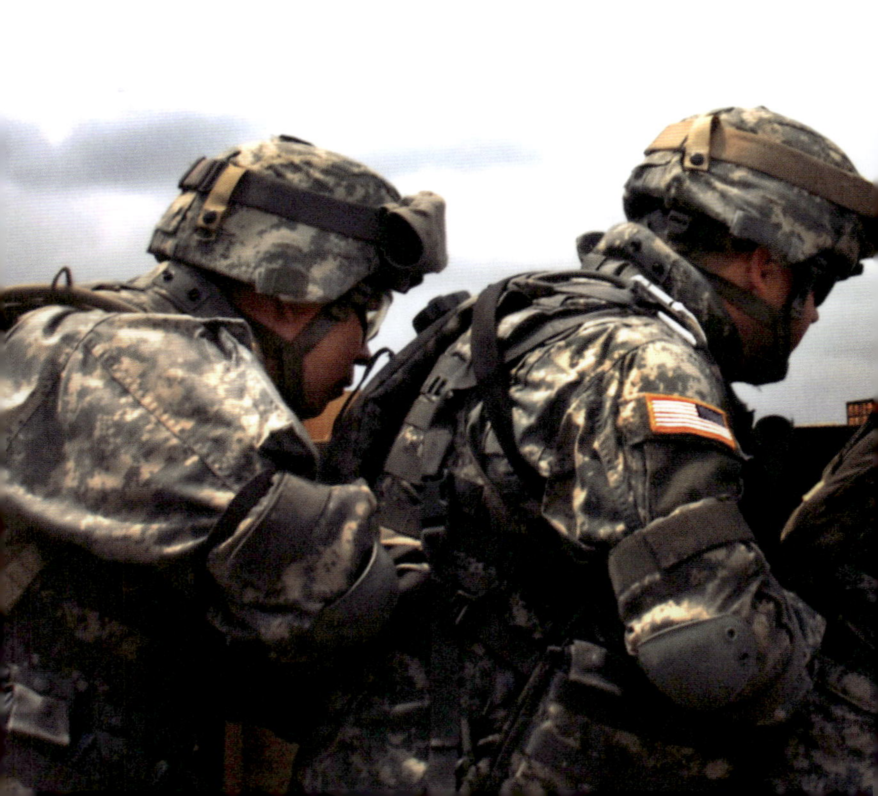

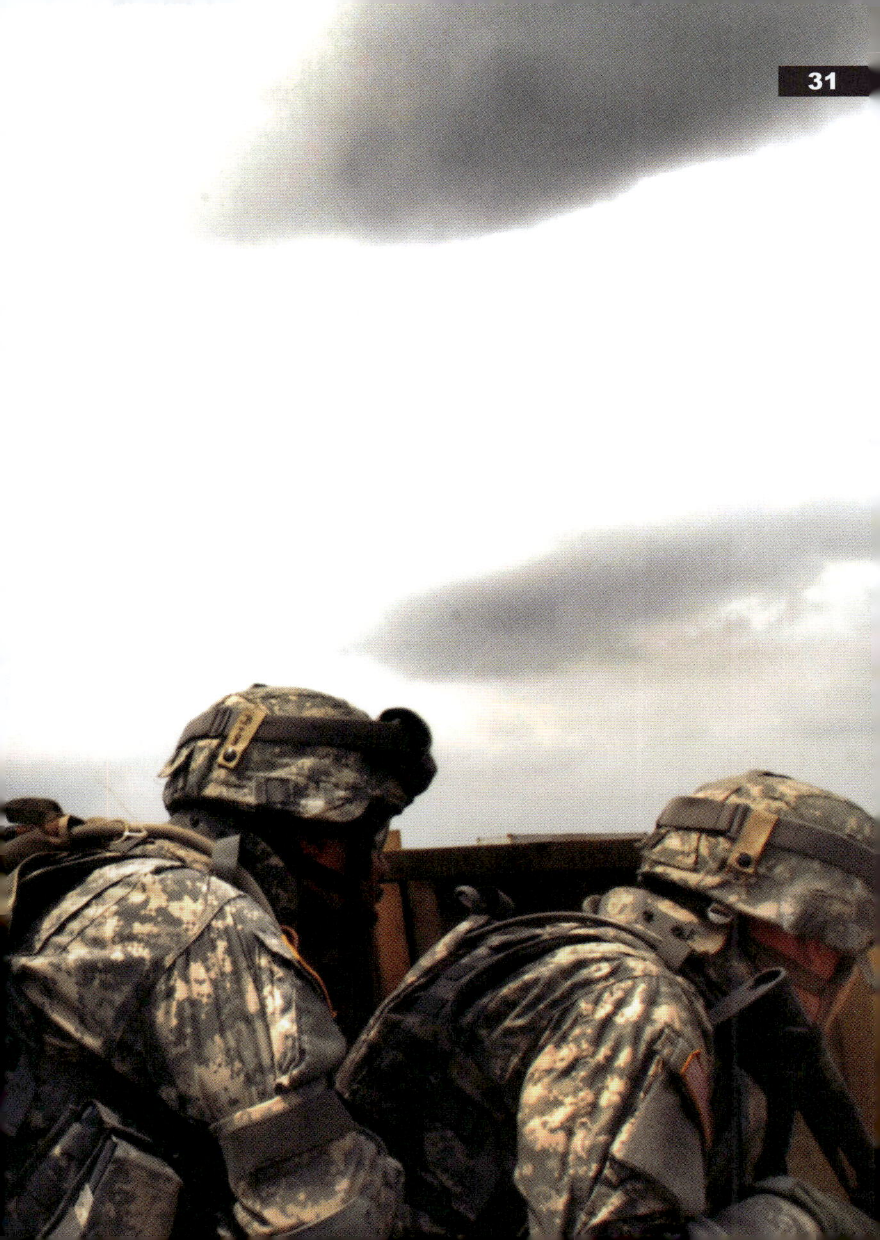

Documentary photography represents reality

rule **10**

In their work, documentary photographers aim to represent reality. Sounds noble enough, but according to acclaimed Mexican photographer Pedro Meyer (1935) it's important to bury this myth, along with the mistaken notion that the camera doesn't lie. "I think it's very important for people to realize that images are not a representation of reality," Meyer says, "the sooner that myth is destroyed and buried, the better for society all around."

———

"It is not a factual photograph per se. The documentary photograph carries with it another thing, a quality in the subject that the artist responds to. It is a photograph which carries the full meaning of the episode or the circumstance or the situation that can only be revealed – because you can't really recapture it – by this other quality. There is no real warfare between the artist and the documentary photographer. He has to be both."
Dorothea Lange (1895-1965), American photographer

"Documentary: That's a sophisticated and misleading word. And not really clear… The term should be documentary style… You see, a document has use, whereas art is really useless."
Walker Evans (1903-1975), American photographer

"Documentary photography is the presentation or representation of an actual fact in a way that makes it credible and vivid to an audience at the time."
David Hurn (1934), British photographer

"I never liked the label documentary photographer. In a visual arts context the expressionist style is the one I feel closest to. But I consider myself simply a photographer."
Markéta Luskačová (1944), Czech photographer

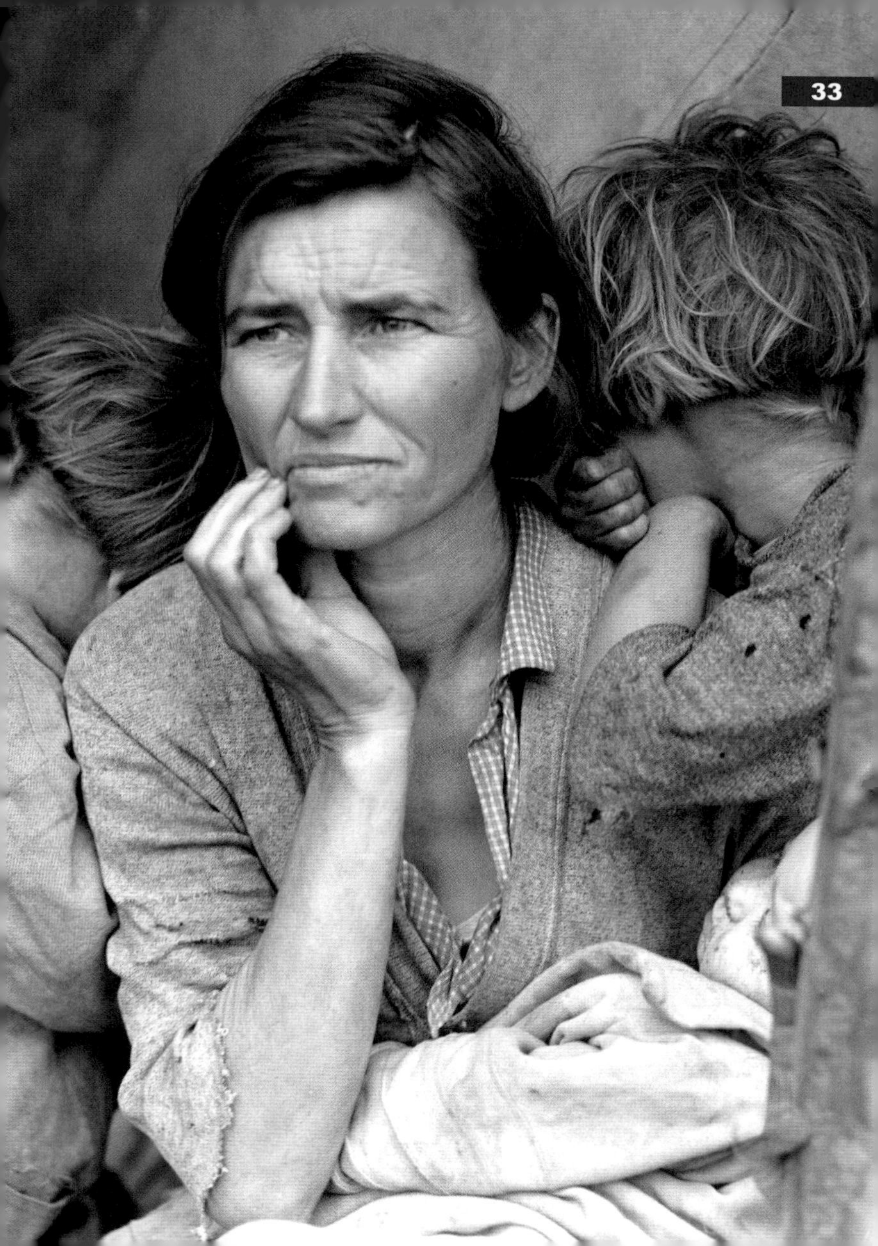

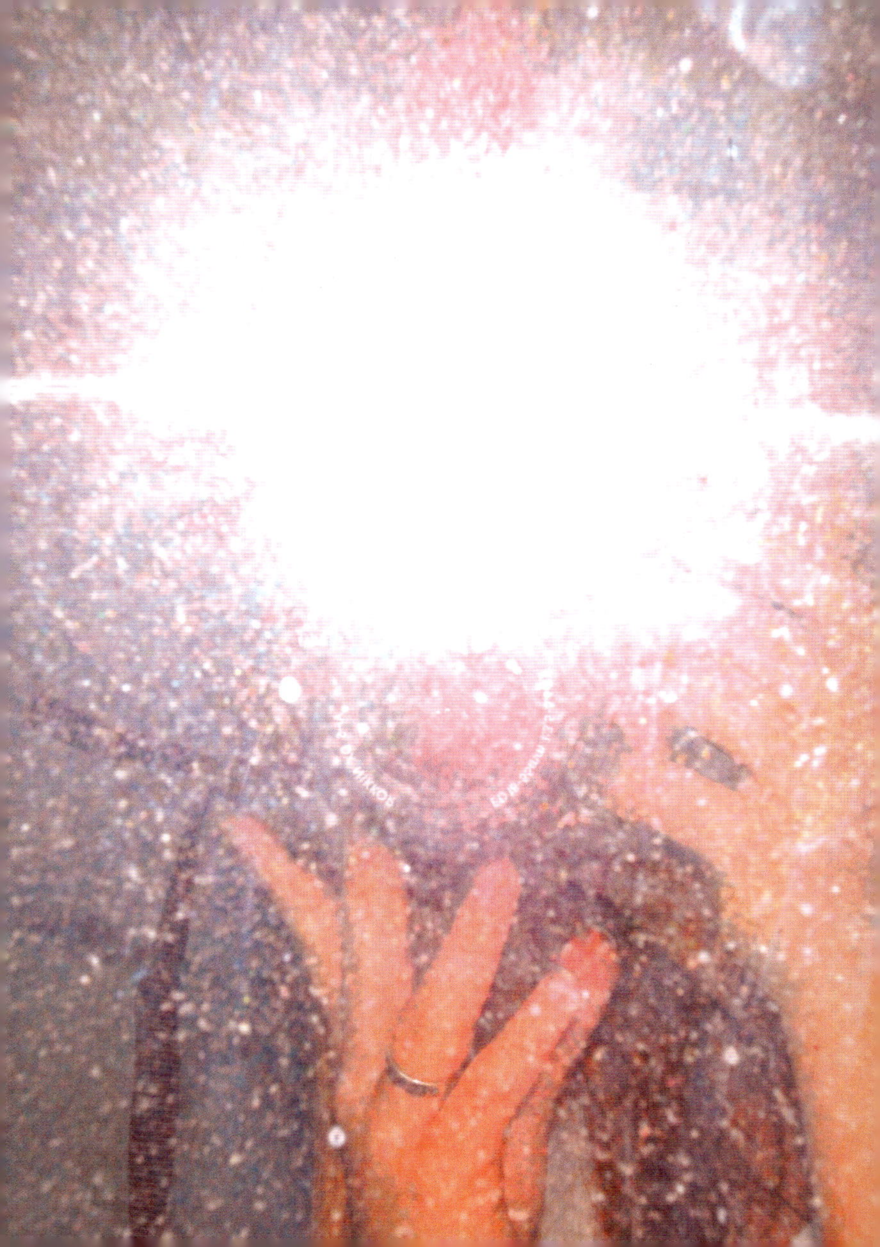

Careful using flash

rule 11

Light is a key component in photography. In the absence of natural light, flash comes in handy. Over the years, different forms of artificial light have been in use – from flash powder to flash bulbs and electronic flashlights – but what hasn't changed is that the wrong use of flash can ruin a perfectly good photo, not to mention temporarily blind the people you're photographing. Simple tricks, such as diffusing the light and keeping proper distance from your subject, can help prevent flash blow-outs.

"Don't use a flash out of respect for the natural lighting, even when there isn't any. If these rules aren't followed, the photographer becomes unbearably obtrusive."
Henri Cartier-Bresson (1908-2004), French photographer

"The flash destroys the secret network of relations that naturally exist between the attentive photographer and his subject."
Henri Cartier-Bresson (1908-2004), French photographer

THE CAMERA DOESN'T LIE

In the nineteenth century the general consensus seemed to be that, in contrast to the more subjective art of painting, photography was a far more objective medium and a photograph an honest representation of reality. Oh, how things have changed. These days you'll be hard pressed to find people who support this claim.

"Photography is a reality so subtle that it becomes more real than reality."
Alfred Stieglitz (1864-1946),
American photographer

"When you see what you express through photography, you realize all the things that can no longer be the object of painting. Why should the artist persist in treating subjects that can be established so clearly with the lens of a camera?"
Pablo Picasso (1881-1973),
Spanish artist

"Only with effort can the camera be forced to lie; basically, it is an honest medium, so the photographer is much more likely to approach nature in a spirit of inquiry, of communion, instead of with the saucy swagger of self-dubbed 'artists'."
Edward Weston (1886-1958),
American photographer

"Not everybody trusts paintings but people believe photographs."
Ansel Adams (1902-1984),
American photographer

"The truth is the best picture, the best propaganda."
Robert Capa (1913-1954),
Hungarian-born American photographer

"All photographs are accurate.
None of them is the truth."
Richard Avedon (1923-2004),
American photographer

"The camera cannot lie, but it
can be an accessory to untruth."
Harold Evans (1928), British
journalist and writer

"Still photographs are the most
powerful weapon in the world. People
believe them, but photographs do lie,
even without manipulation. They are
only half-truths."
Eddie Adams (1933-2004), American
photographer and photojournalist

"No individual photo explains
anything. That's what makes
photography such a wonderful
and problematic medium. It is the
photographer's job to get this
medium to say what you need it
to say. Because photography has
a certain verisimilitude, it has gained
a currency as truthful – but photographs
have always been convincing lies."
Joel Sternfeld (1944), American
photographer

"I can't describe reality; at the most,
I can try to capture things that seem
to be valid, the way I see them."
Anders Petersen (1944), Swedish
photographer

"You don't have to sort of enhance
reality. There is nothing stranger than
truth."
Annie Leibovitz (1949), American
photographer

"A photo is always a kind of lie. Truth
is only present for a matter of a fraction
of a second."
Rineke Dijkstra (1959), Dutch
photographer

"People say photographs don't lie,
mine do."
David LaChapelle (1963), American
photographer

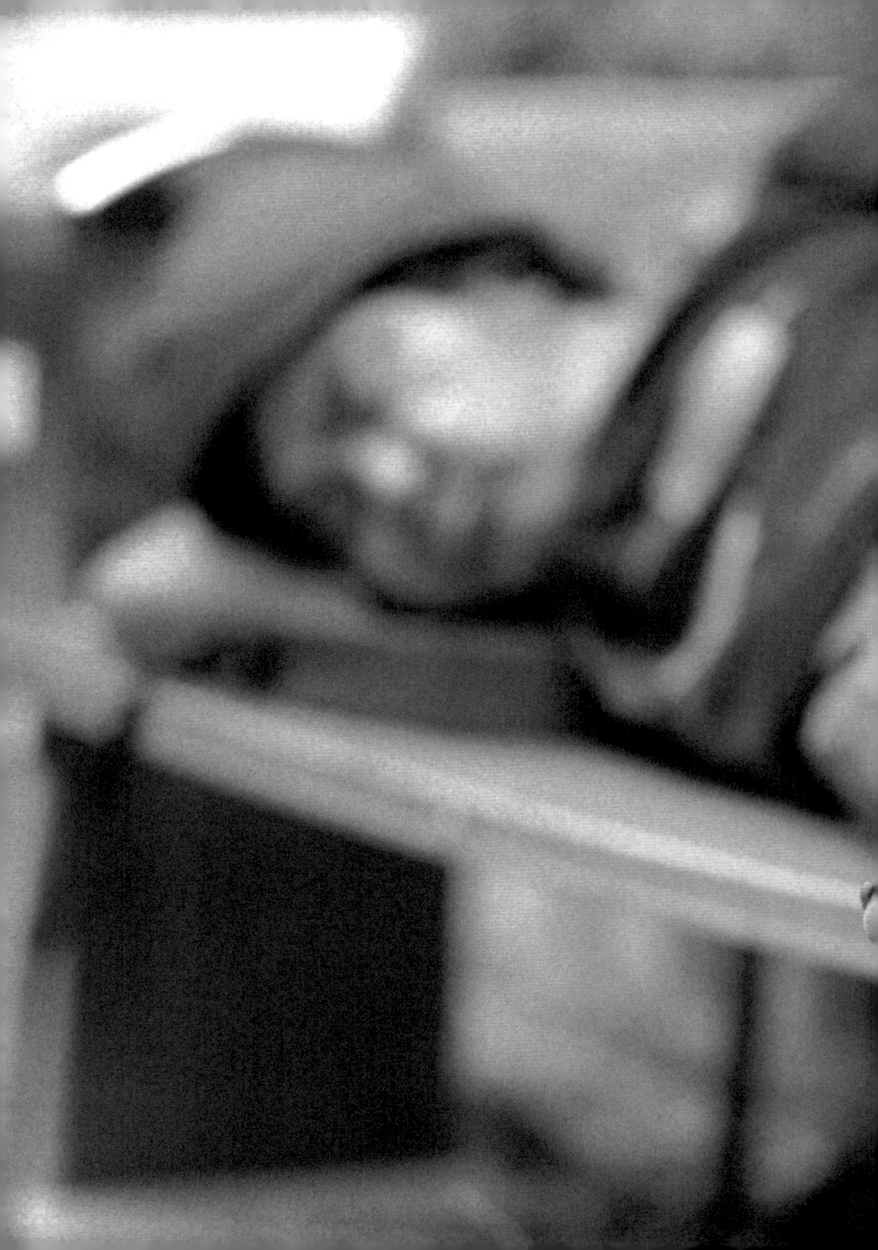

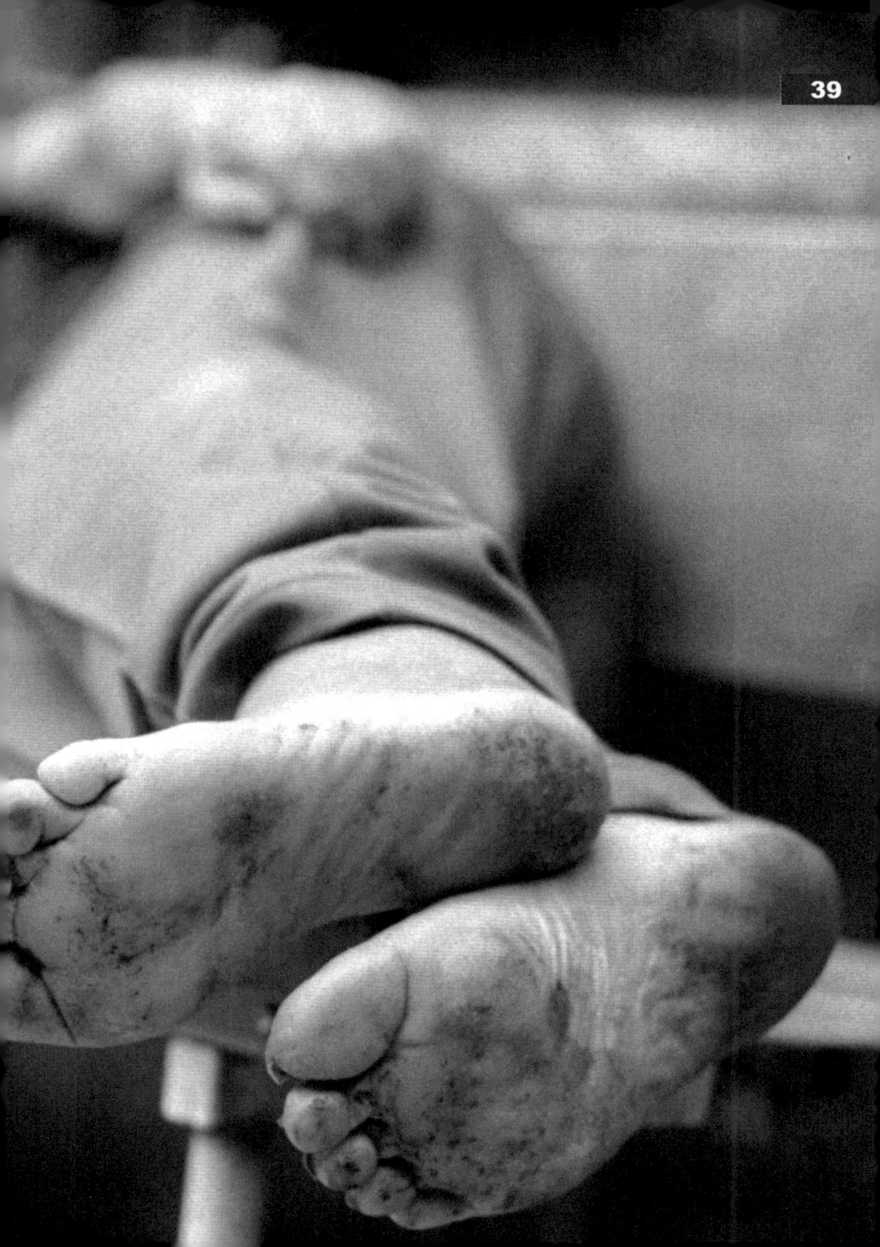

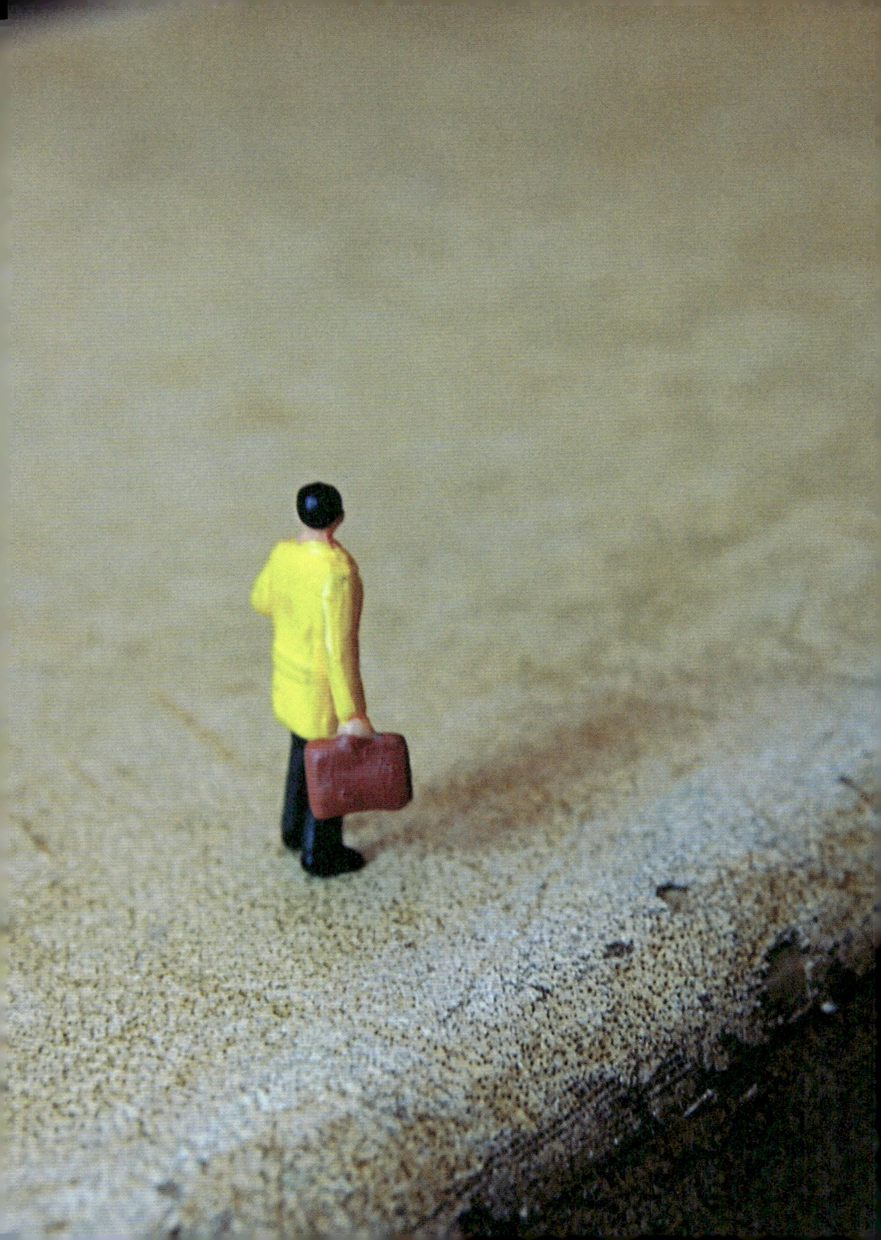

Find your angle

rule
13

Photography is a great storytelling medium, a way to show or tell something from a certain perspective, both literally and figuratively. Different angles create different perspectives and in turn alter the story you're telling. Shoot from eye level and you'll end up with relatively neutral images, while close-ups add drama. Find the angle that helps tell your story.

———

"I seldom think when I take a picture. My eyes and fingers react – click. But first, it's most important to decide on the angle at which your photograph is to be taken."
Alfred Eisenstaedt (1898-1995),
German-born American photographer

"There is a lot of talk about camera angles; but the only valid angles in existence are the angles of the geometry of composition and not the ones fabricated by the photographer who falls flat on his stomach or performs other antics to procure his effects."
Henri Cartier-Bresson (1908-2004),
French photographer

Get some good shoes

In the book 'On Being A Photographer' Bill Jay and Magnum photographer David Hurn give tips to budding photographers. One of their most practical advices, and arguably the most surprising one, is to invest in a decent pair of shoes. Many a photographer spends a great deal of time and money on getting the right gear, but while a good camera and a decent pair of lenses are important tools in any photographer's kit, so are a pair of comfortable shoes. "If you become a photographer, you will do a lot of walking, so buy good shoes," says Hurn. The perfect pair is described as "rugged, durable, suitable for all terrain and weather" and "so comfortable they can be walked in all day," yet "smart enough that [they] can be worn with a suit to a posh event."

"Put your camera around your neck along with putting on your shoes, and there it is, an appendage of the body that shares your life with you."
Dorothea Lange (1895-1965), American photographer

"Get a good pair of walking shoes and... fall in love."
Abbas (1944), Iranian photographer

"A photographer may not just walk the streets but he/she does a lot of walking, with a purpose, so the most important piece of equipment after the camera is a good pair of shoes. A writer can do a lot of work from a hotel room but a photographer has to be there, so he/she is in for a hell of a lot of hiking."
David Hurn (1934), British photographer

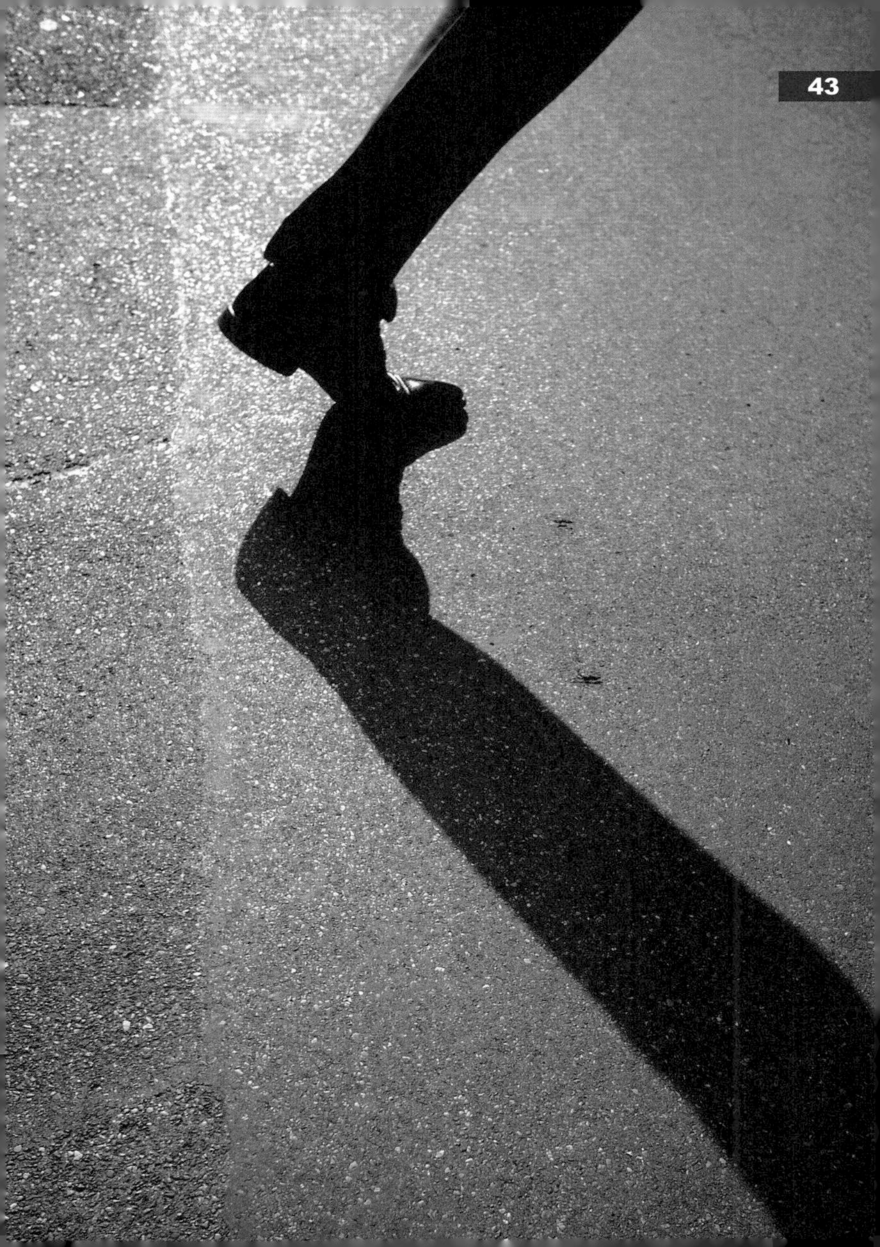
43

Don't be afraid to fail

When embarking on a creative or artistic undertaking, failure is always an option. But don't let the possibility of future failure dampen your enthusiasm. After all, fear is the death of creativity. Or to quote American scientist and co-founder of the Polaroid company Edwin Herbert Land (1909-1991): "The essential part of creativity is not being afraid to fail."

———

"Ultimately, success or failure in photographing people depends on the photographer's ability to understand his fellow man."
Edward Weston (1886-1958),
American photographer

"Ever tried. Ever failed. No matter. Try again. Fail again. Fail better."
Samuel Beckett (1906-1989), Irish
playwright, poet and writer

"I think that basically all of my photographs are failures... I'm not saying that as a self-negation or anything like that, I just don't judge it upon how 'good' it was, but rather how I'd failed upon what I was trying to say..."
W. Eugene Smith (1918-1978),
American photographer

In recent years, the market has been flooded with affordable good-quality, semi-professional cameras, as well as apps that are able to produce retro-inspired, albeit generic-looking, pictures. This development has certainly helped to democratize and further popularize the medium of photography but unfortunately it has also instilled the somewhat misguided, but certainly controversial, idea that the mere ownership of a DSLR camera or Instagram-like app makes you a photographer.

———

"No photographer is as good as the simplest camera."
Edward Steichen (1879-1973), American photographer

"When I first started learning how to take photographs, you had to spend the first six months figuring out what an f-stop was. Now you just go and take pictures. Nobody thinks about technical issues anymore because cameras or camera phones take care of that automatically."
Martin Parr (1952), British photographer

"Instagram is debasing real photography. The Instagram/Hipstamatic/Snapseed filters are the antithesis of creativity, and make all pictures look the same."
Kate Bevan, British writer and broadcaster

"You could make an analogy to the advent of the electric guitar or electronic music. Much to the annoyance of classical musicians, those things made 'everyone' a musician. I grew up on punk rock, hip hop and death metal, so I welcome the post-classical age of photography, and the explosion of amateur expression that comes with it... Obviously, it sucks to be a professional photographer, and it's personally inconvenient to lose your pedestal and your livelihood to a $2 app, but that doesn't mean it's a bad thing for photography."
Teru Kuwayama (1970), American photographer

Instagram does not make you a photographer

"My own Flickr account has a fair few images that look like they could have been created with Instagram's retro-flavored algorithms. They weren't - they are all film. They are the result of a decade and a half's mistakes and mis-steps. Cross-processed slide film with wild color shifts. Grainy, muted colors on out-of-date film. Flare and faded colors on lenses made without modern, contrast-boosting coatings. The mistakes, however, made me a better photographer. And the moments when it does somehow come together (...) made the perspiration worth it."
Stephen Dowling (1973), British photographer

"We worked really hard to make it easy for people to share their lives in a beautiful way. It is one thing to share a photo; it's another for that photo to look gorgeous."
Kevin Systrom (1984), American entrepreneur and co-founder of Instagram

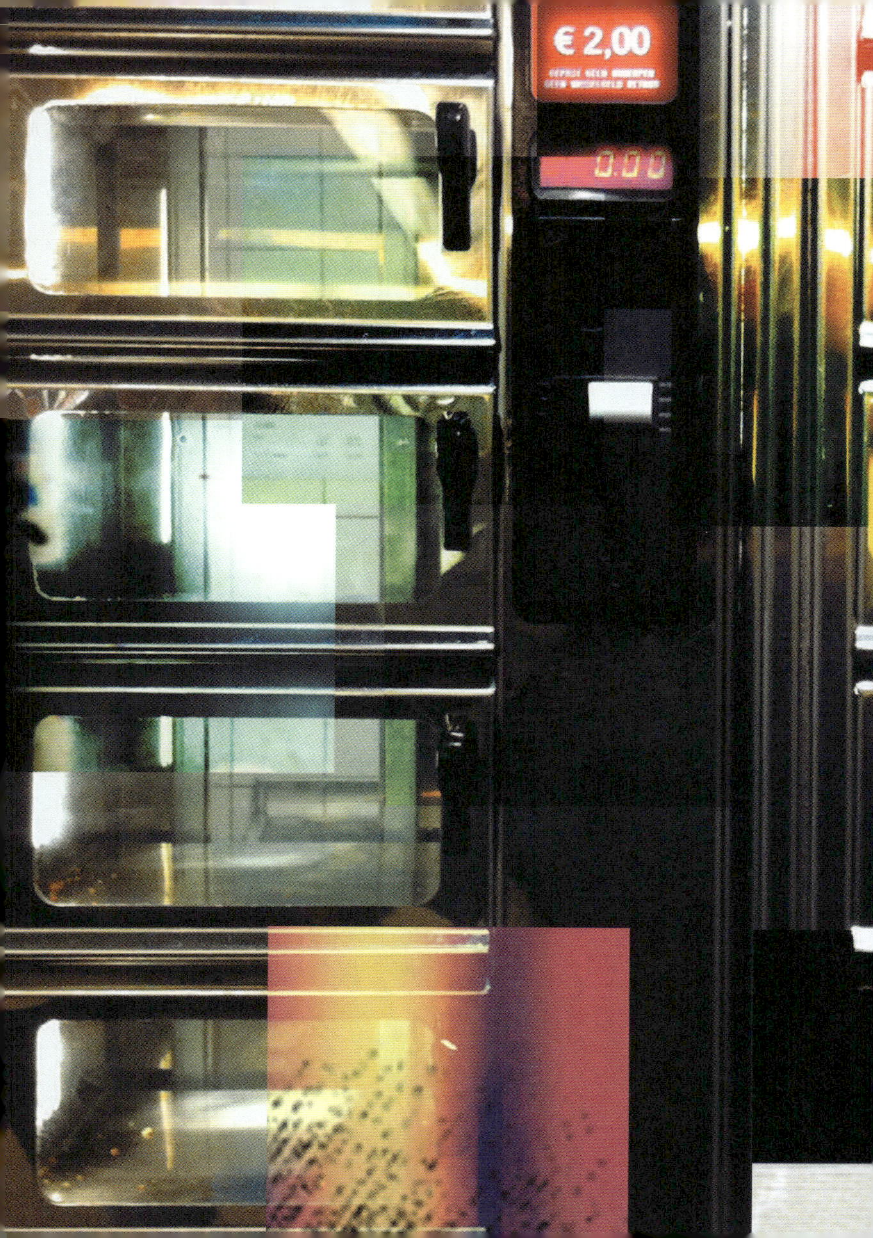

€ 2,00
GEPAST GELD INWERPEN
GEEN WISSELGELD RETOUR
0.00

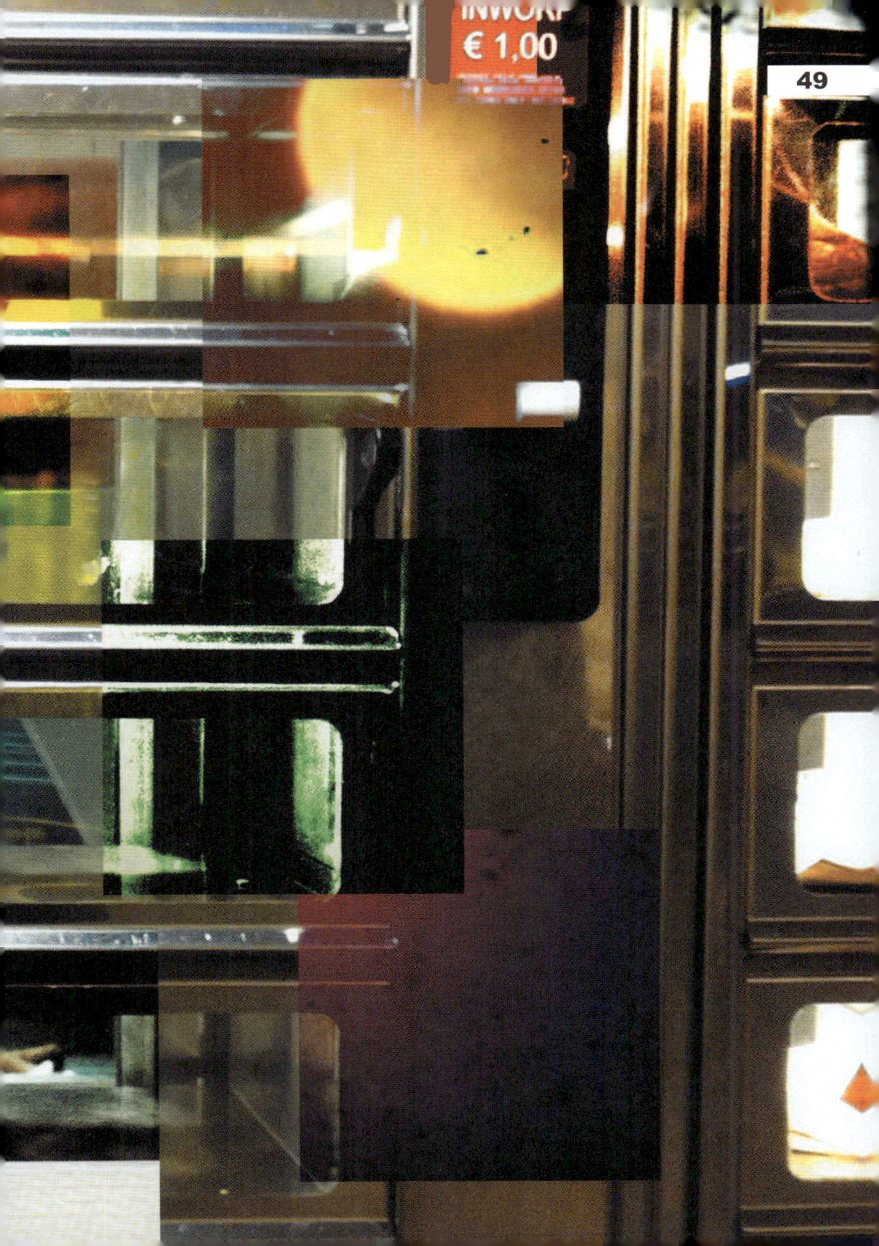
INWORP
€ 1,00

Get close

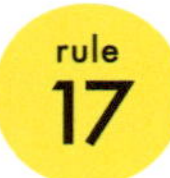

The legendary war photographer Robert Capa (1913-1954) famously said that "if your pictures aren't good enough, you aren't close enough." Capa, who also was one of the founding fathers of Magnum Photos, took his own advice to heart, reporting directly from the front line. In the end, Capa got a little too close: he was tragically killed in 1954 when he stepped on a landmine while on assignment in Indochina.

———

"I never use a telephoto lens. I need to be close to people. I need their complicity; I need them to be aware that I am there taking their picture. I hate paparazzi."
Graciela Iturbide (1942), Mexican photographer

"My lens of choice was always the 35 mm. It was more environmental. You can't come in closer with the 35 mm."
Annie Leibovitz (1949), American photographer

"I go straight in, very close to people and I do that because it's the only way you can get the picture. You go right up to them. Even now, I don't find it easy. I don't announce it. I pretend to be focusing elsewhere."
Martin Parr (1952), British photographer

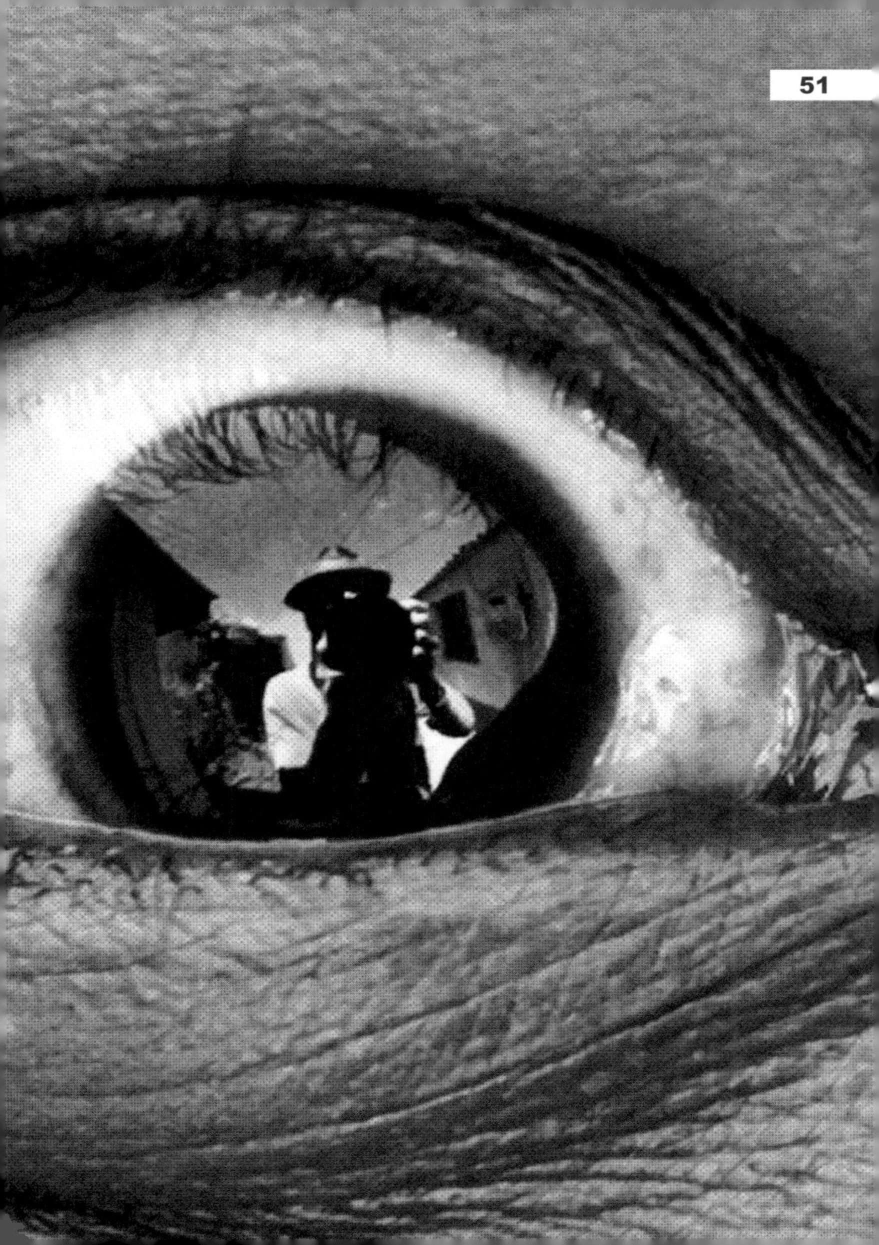

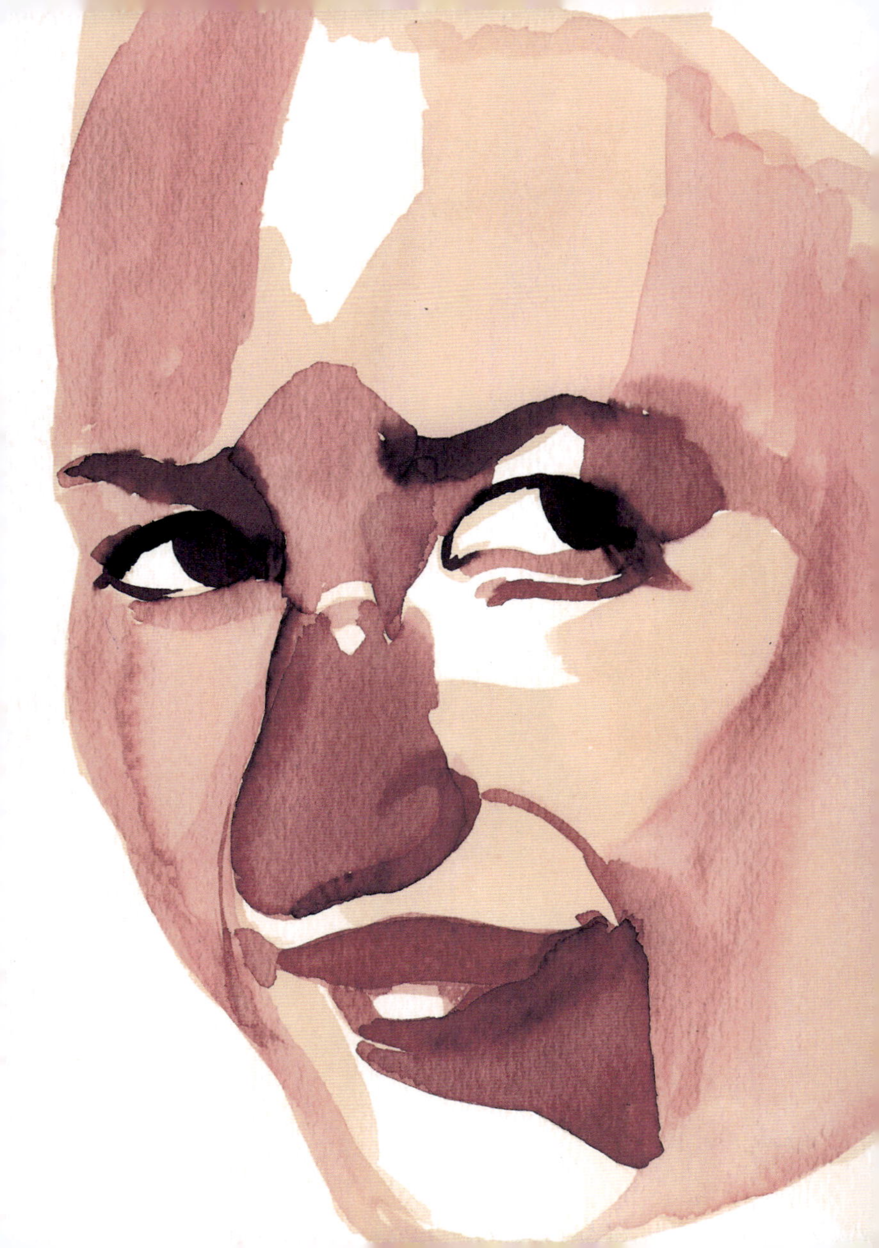

Find your muse

Forget about finding your inner muse, get your inspiration from a real-life one instead.

———

"I am, and forever will be, devastated by the gift of Audrey Hepburn before my camera. I cannot lift her to greater heights. She is already there. I can only record. I cannot interpret her. There is no going further than who she is. She has achieved in herself her ultimate portrait."
Richard Avedon (1923-2004),
American photographer

"He just liked to take the pictures of me. In every pose. Rain or shine. And whatever I was doing. If I was doing the dishes or if I was half asleep. And he knew that I never, never said no. I was always there for him. Because I knew that Harry would only do the right thing."
Eleanor Callahan (1935-2012),
wife and muse of photographer Harry
Callahan

"A muse is anything but a paid model. The muse in her purest aspect is the feminine part of the male artist, with which he must have intercourse if he is to bring into being a new work. She is the anima to his animus, the yin to his yang, except that, in a reversal of gender roles, she penetrates or inspires him and he gestates and brings forth, from the womb of the mind."
Germaine Greer (1939), Australian
journalist

"There have been so many moments of collaboration, both intense and ebullient, allowing me to experience a sense of being a muse, a hot shot, or merely myself."
Patti Smith (1946), American singer

"Never work with animals or children."

Pictures of cuddly animals and cute kids tend to pull on the heart strings. However, as this (in)famous quote by American actor and comedian W.C. Fields (1880-1946) aptly points out, getting the money shot while working with these young and rambunctious models tends to require plenty of patience and hard work on the part of the photographer. That and a bit of luck.

———

"I have a deep love and respect for children and I cannot imagine photographic life without them playing a major part. I hope that through my work as a photographer, I have been able to pass on my appreciation of their beauty and charm."
Anne Geddes (1956), Australian photographer

"I enjoy working with children because they are genuine; they don't wear masks."
Loretta Lux (1969), German artist

"I love working with children, however, you do need to have patience, because it can take some time to get what you are after, and sometimes it just doesn't work. It usually works when I'm photographing a child who has an intuitive understanding of what I'm trying to achieve. As for animals... that is hard work! They are tricky to direct."
Petrina Hicks (1972), Australian photographer

"My Weimaraners are perfect fashion models. Their elegant, slinky forms are covered in gray - and gray, as everyone knows, goes with anything."
William Wegman (1943), American artist and photographer, best known for his photographs of dogs

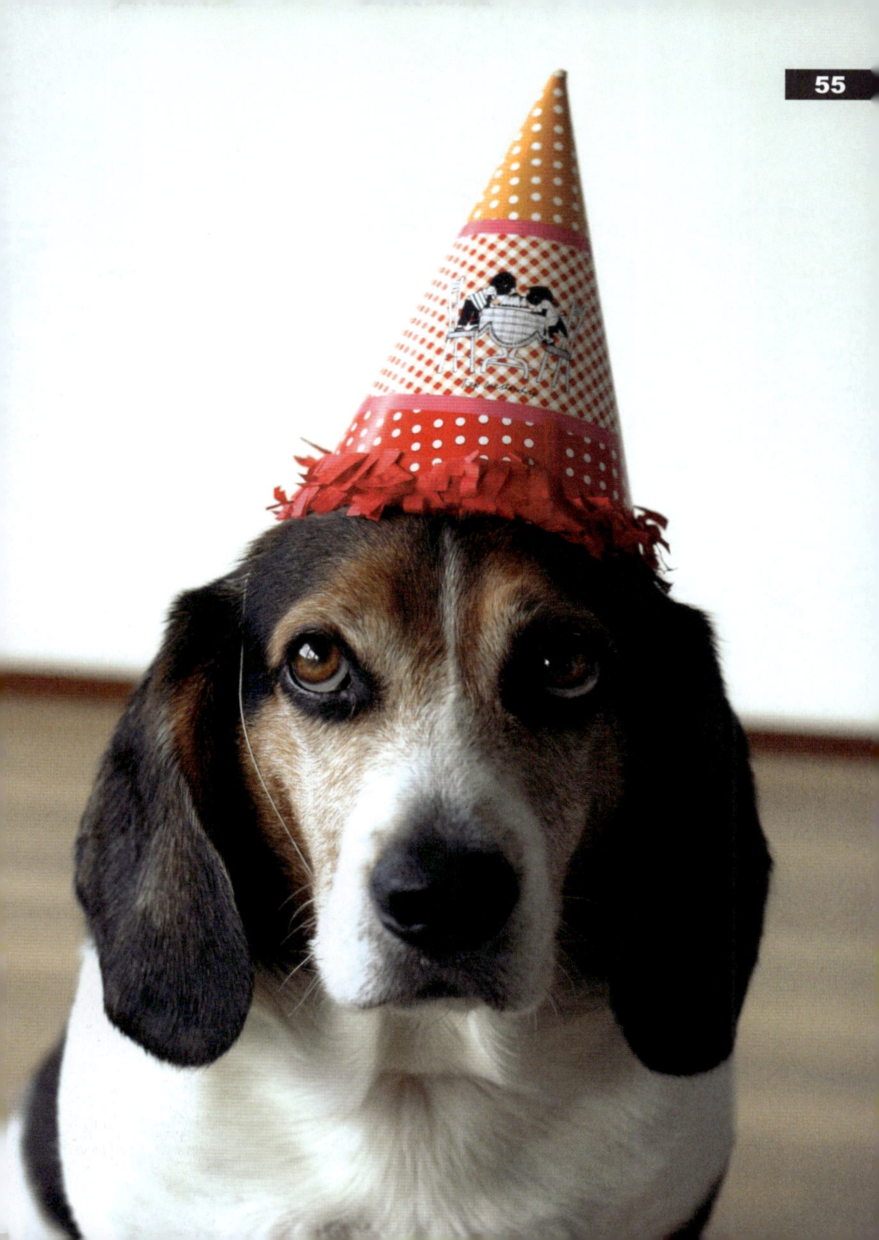

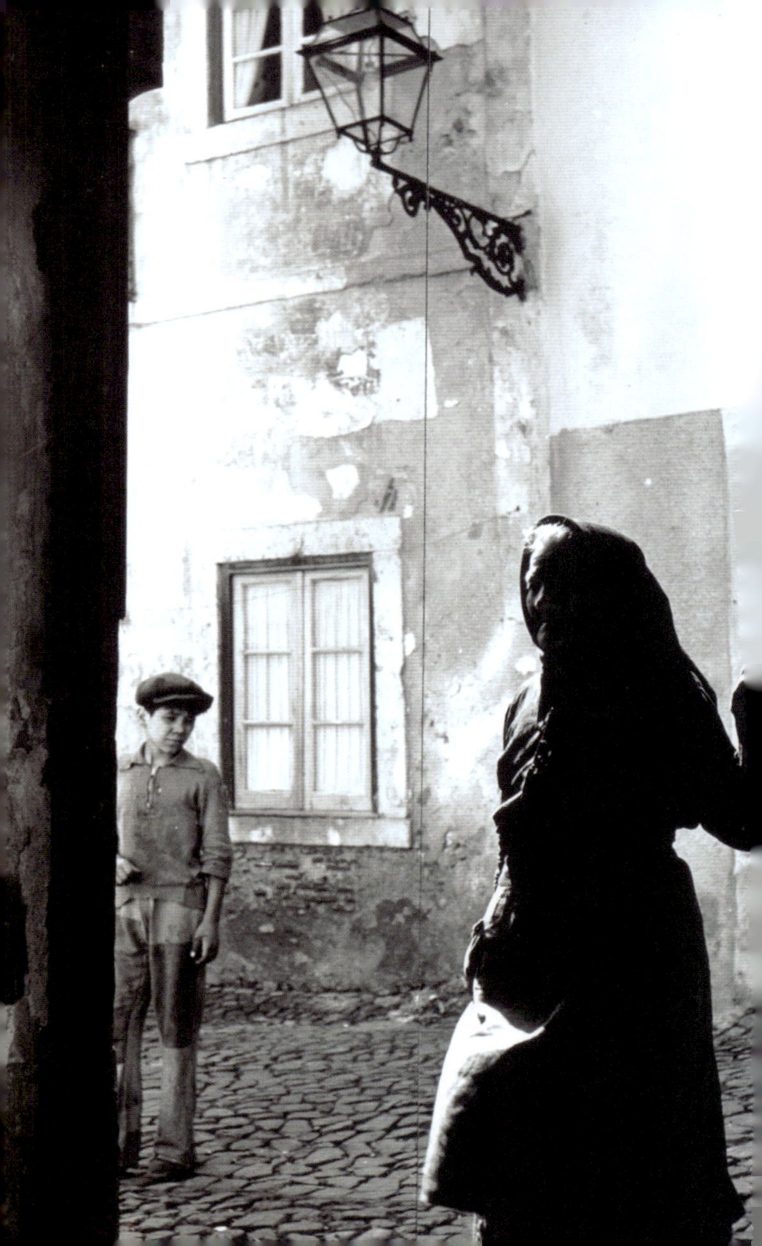

"BLACK AND WHITE ARE THE COLORS OF PHOTOGRAPHY."

Up to the 1960s and 70s, color photography had something of a bad rep. Indeed, as British design critic and writer Rick Poynor points out "color was identified with commerce, with manipulative advertising and crowd-pleasing stories about the stars in popular magazines," which is why "serious photographers" preferred to shoot the world in black and white. American photographer Robert Frank even went as far as to declare that "black and white are the colors of photography." While the resistance to color photography has certainly faded, Frank's words still resonate with certain photography purists who to this day believe that color photography is the domain of both commercial and amateur photography.

———————

"Color photography is vulgar."
Walker Evans (1903-1975), American photographer

"When you photograph people in color, you photograph their clothes. But when you photograph people in black and white, you photograph their souls!"
Ted Grant (1929), Canadian photographer

"Black and white are the colors of photography. To me they symbolize the alternatives of hope and despair to which mankind is forever subjected. Most of my photographs are of people; they are seen simply, as through the eyes of the man in the street. There is one thing the photograph must contain, the humanity of the moment. This kind of photography is realism. But realism is not enough – there has to be vision, and the two together can make a good photograph. It is difficult to describe this thin line where matter ends and mind begins."
Robert Frank (1924), American photographer and film director

"Color is everything, black and white is more."
Dominic Rouse (1959), British photographer

CROP WELL

rule **21**

If you failed to frame your image on site or set, the good old crop tool can come in handy and will enhance composition and cut out any unwanted details.

———————

"With the camera, it's all or nothing. You either get what you're after at once, or what you do has to be worthless. I don't think the essence of photography has the hand in it so much. The essence is done very quietly with a flash of the mind, and with a machine. I think too that photography is editing, editing after the taking. After knowing what to take, you have to do the editing."
Walker Evans (1903-1975), American photographer

"[I crop] for the benefit of the pictures. The world just does not fit conveniently into the format of a 35mm camera."
W. Eugene Smith (1918-1978), American photographer

"My pictures can be cropped so long as their meaning remains intact. The one thing I will not tolerate is mindless misrepresentation for reasons of layout."
Yann Arthus Bertrand (1946), French photographer

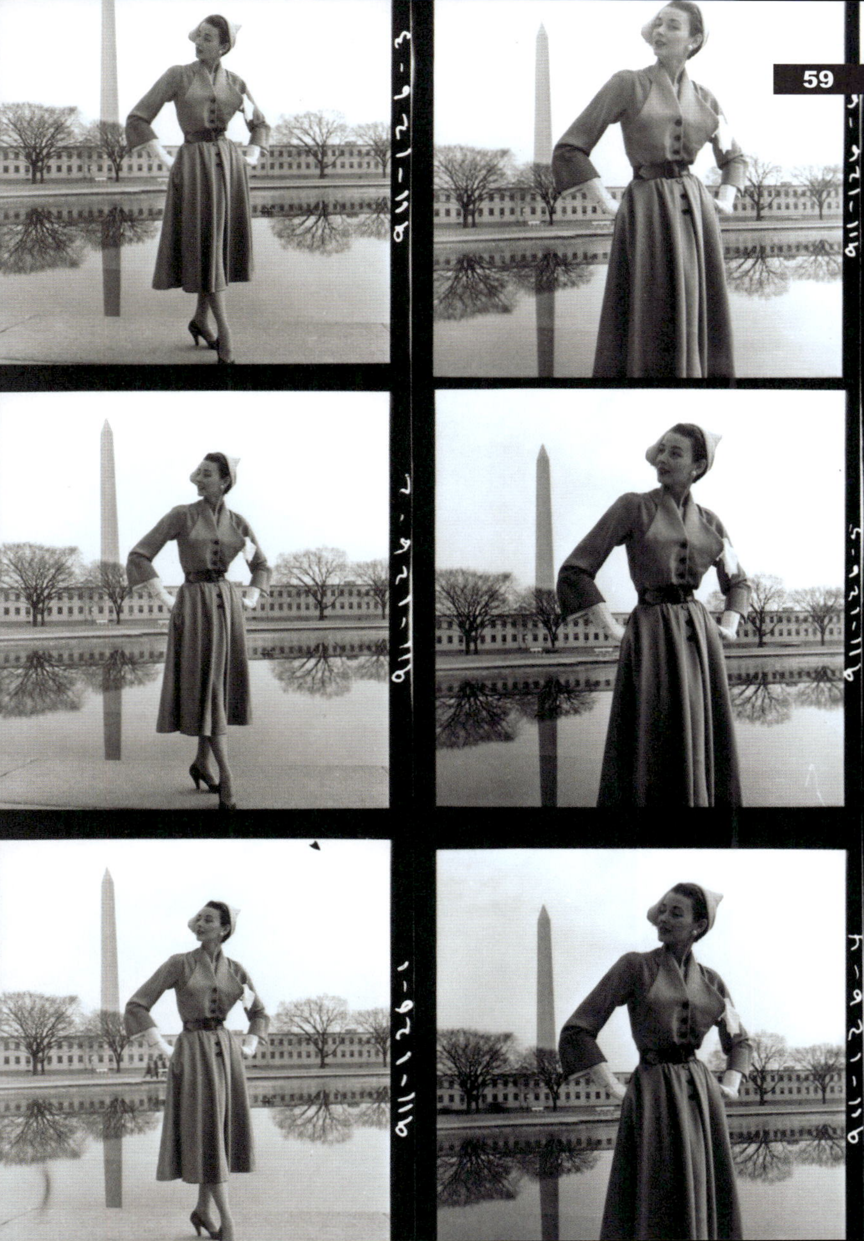

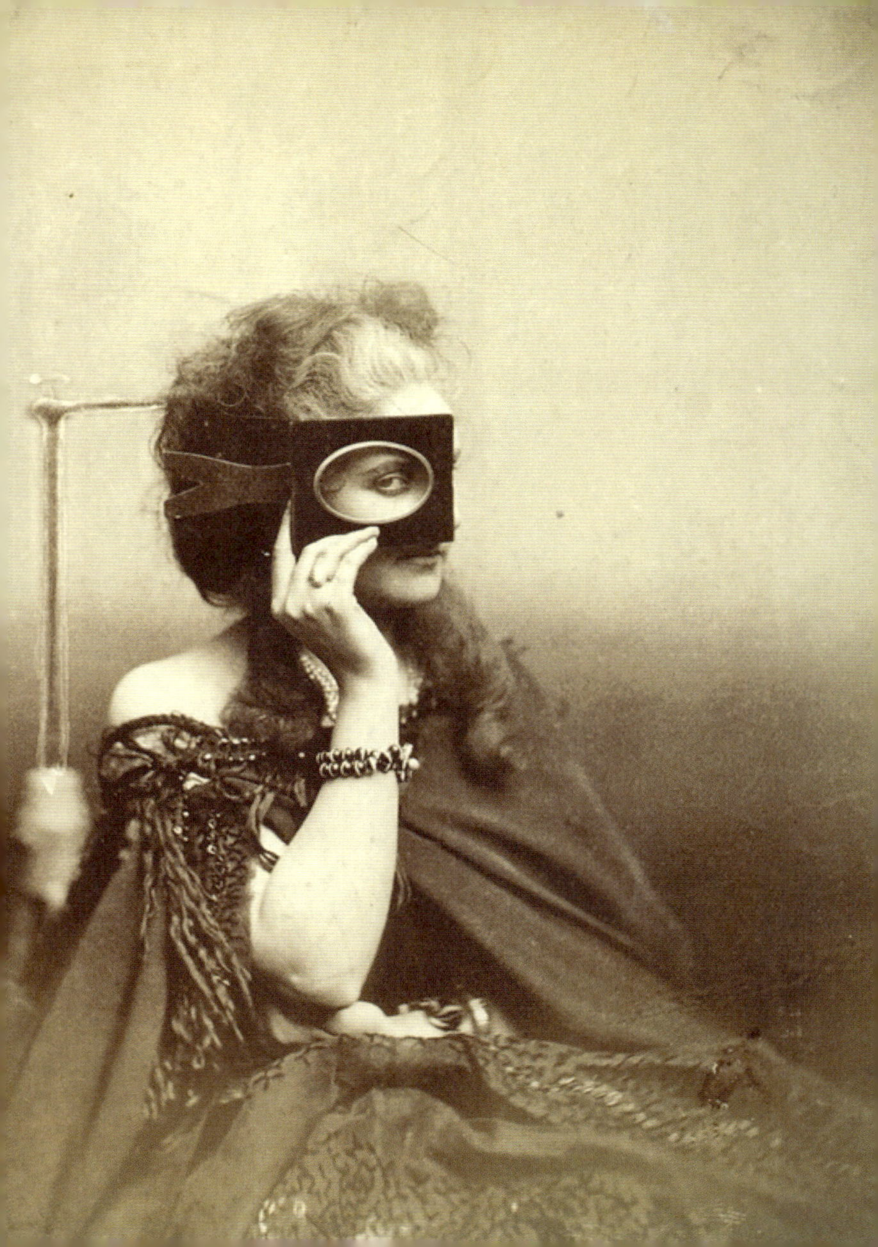

"Fashion is a photograph."

British graphic designer Peter Saville (1955) has stated that fashion is a photograph, arguing that "when we think of fashion we think of a photograph." Virginia Oldoini, aka the Countess of Castiglione (1837-1899), was instrumental in linking the worlds of fashion and photography. Sometimes referred to as the world's first fashion model, Oldoini was more than a little obsessed with her own appearance. She turned to French photographer Pierre-Louise Pierson (1822 - 1913) who took over 400 pictures of the Countess in his Paris studio in elaborate costumes. But fashion photography really came into its own once fashion magazines started placing photos in their publications. A tradition that continues to this day.

———————

"What I find interesting is working in a society with certain taboos – and fashion photography is about that kind of society. To have taboos, then to get around them – that is interesting."
Helmut Newton (1920-2004),
German-Australian photographer

"There's always been a separation between fashion and what I call my 'deeper' work. Fashion is where I make my living. I'm not knocking it. It's a pleasure to make a living that way. It's pleasure, and then there's the deeper pleasure of doing my portraits."
Richard Avedon (1923-2004),
American photographer

"I never cared for fashion much, amusing little seams and witty little pleats: it was the girls I liked."
David Bailey (1938), British
photographer

"I honestly don't read fashion magazines. Anyway, fashion magazines don't contain fashion. They just con-tain lifestyle, and it's all to do with photography and not to do with actual clothes anymore."
Vivienne Westwood (1941), British
fashion designer

A picture is worth a thousand words

This well-known saying first popped up in 1921 when 'Printers' Ink', an advertising trade journal, ran an article by Fred R. Barnard on the use of images on streetcars as a form of advertisement. The piece read: "One Look is Worth A Thousand Words." Six years later, Barnard used the saying in another ad, slightly changing it into "One Picture is Worth Ten Thousand Words." The slogan stuck and a 'ridiculous' rule was born.

———————

"If I could tell the story in words, I wouldn't need to lug around a camera."
Lewis Hine (1874-1940), American photographer

"I don't think it's necessary to put your feelings about photography in words. I've read things that photographers have written for exhibitions and so forth about their subjective feelings about photography and mostly I think it's disturbing. I think they're fooling themselves very often. They're just talking, they're not saying anything."
Eliot Porter (1901-1990), American photographer

"A true photograph need not be explained, nor can it be contained in words."
Ansel Adams (1902-1984), American photographer

"If you don't have anything to say, your photographs are not going to say much."
Gordon Parks (1912-2006), American photographer, writer and director

"A picture says more than a thousand words, only as much as a thousand words say more than a picture. A thousand apples don't taste any better than a pear, and a thousand pears don't taste any better than an apple. The apple tastes different to the pear, no matter how many of them there are. A thousand words say something different to a picture."
Bo Bergström (1946), Swedish author, lecturer and creative director

"I don't trust words. I trust pictures."
Gilles Peress (1946), French photojournalist

"There must be a reason why photographers are not very good at verbal communication. I think we get lazy."
Annie Leibovitz (1949), American photographer

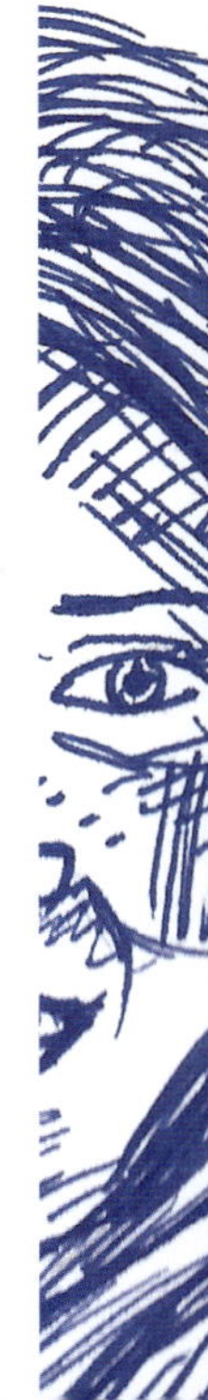

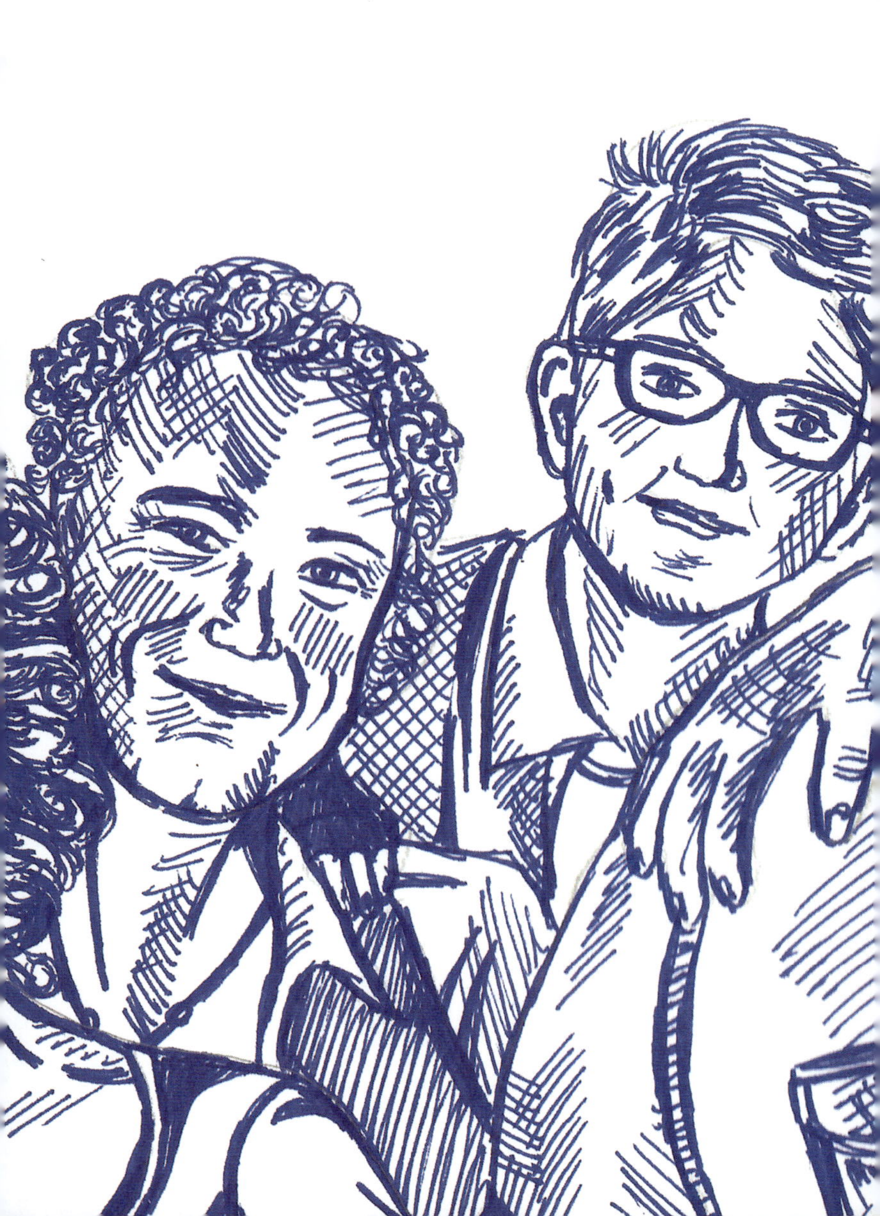

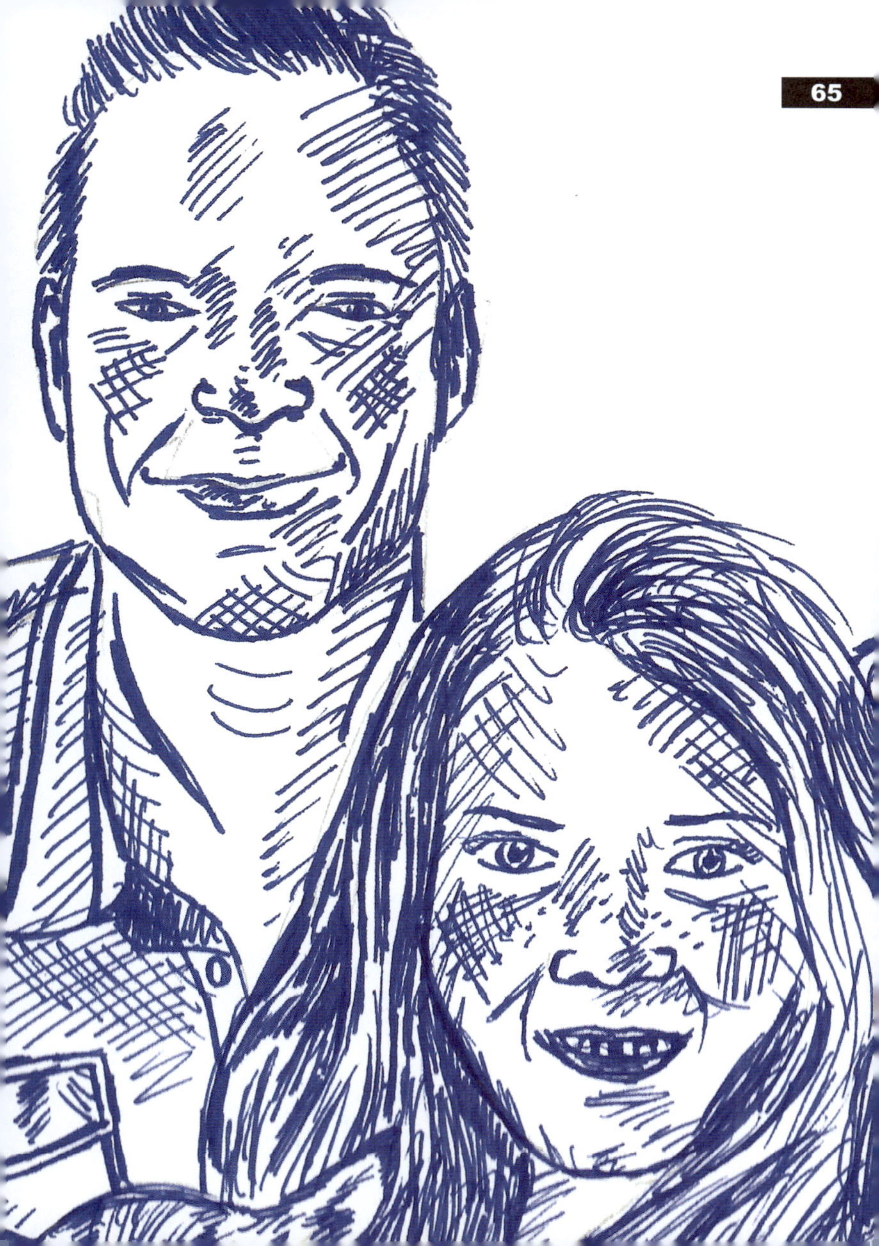

Frame your image

A little post-production on your photo goes a long way. But while the crop tool has made the life of photographers a lot easier, there's still the old viewfinder to fall back on. Or, if you want to go really low-tech, the old hand frame.

———

"In order to 'give a meaning' to the world, one has to feel oneself involved in what he frames through the viewfinder."
Henri Cartier-Bresson (1908-2004), French photographer

"By making a frame you're being selective, then you edit the pictures you want published and you're being selective again. You develop a point of view that you want to express. You try to go into a situation with an open mind, but then you form an opinion, and you express it in your photographs."
Mary Ellen Mark (1940), American photographer

"For a long time I've lived with the inadequacy of that frame to tell everything I knew, and I think a lot about what is outside of the frame…"
Susan Meiselas (1948), American photographer

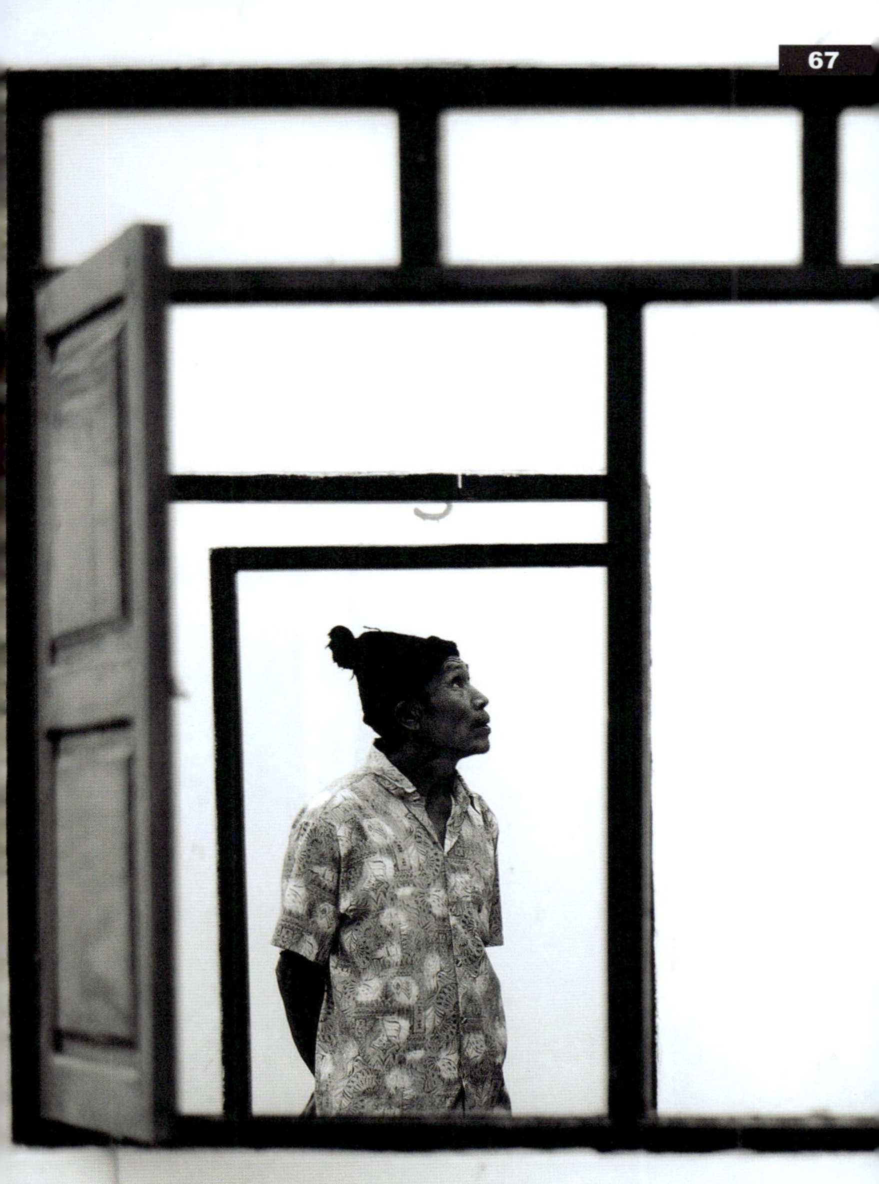

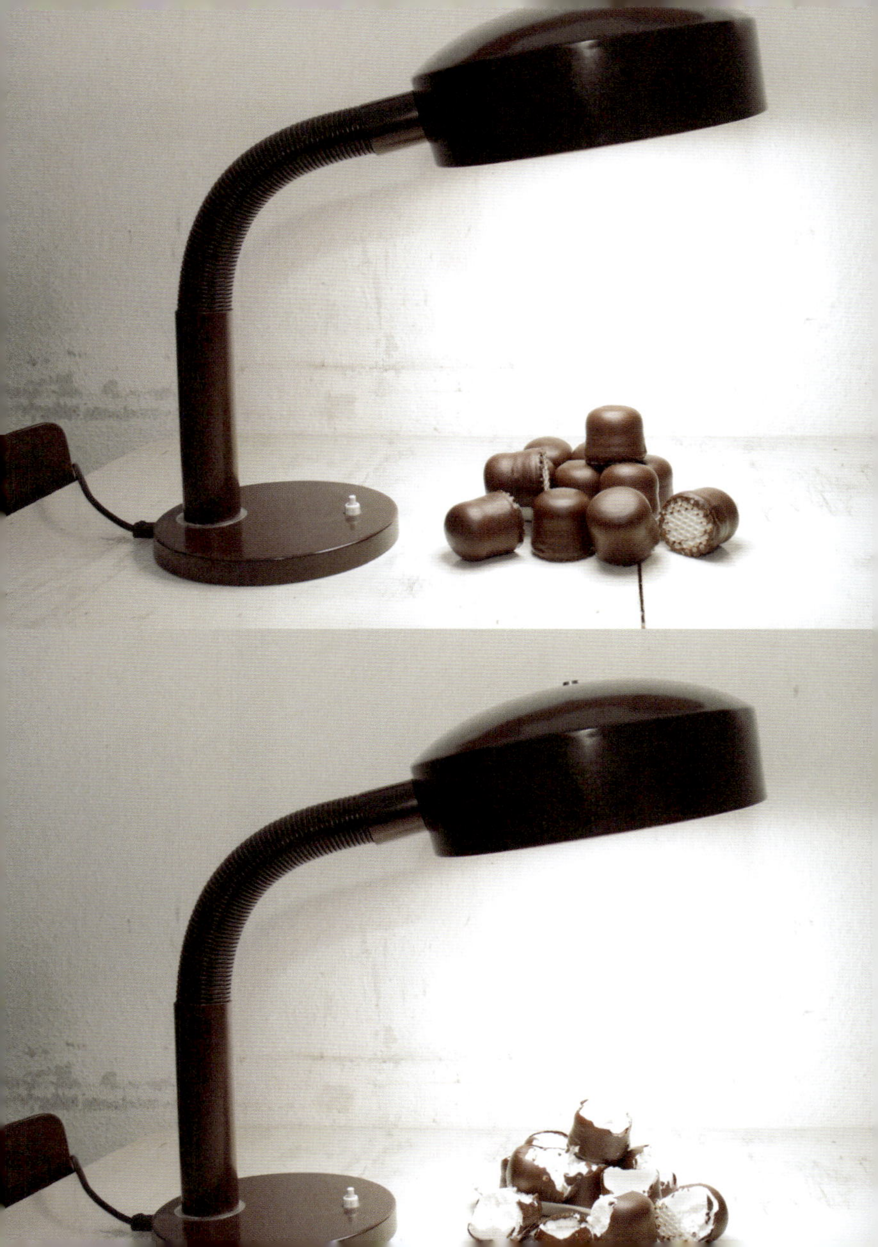

Never photograph people eating

rule 25

In 2010 The New York Times ran a piece in which the photographer and food stylist Andrew Scrivani explained in great detail why you should never photograph people eating. "First off, people make funny faces when they eat. Mouths agape, eyes squinting or bugging out, tongues wagging, it's not a pretty sight," Scrivani wrote, "[And] if you must have an eating shot, I suggest shooting the children. Children eating can be genuinely cute and funny. They are messy and awkward and it retains its appropriateness. Adults eating in freeze frame can just be plain disturbing at times. Years of shooting editorially, in restaurants, made me realize just how hard it can be to find a suitable picture for publication that would not embarrass your subjects."

PAPARAZZI ARE NOT PHOTOGRAPHERS

In his 1960 classic 'La Dolce Vita' Italian director Federico Fellini first introduced the term 'paparazzi'. The movie, which depicts a week in the life of a tabloid reporter, also features a photographer colleague by the name of Paparazzo. The name stuck and to this day celeb-stalking photographers the world over are known as paparazzi, a derogative term that hints at the disdain felt towards these image hunters by 'real' photographers and celebrities alike.

———————

"Celebrities were quick to understand that paparazzi could make icons of them. The more a star is followed and admired, the greater the adulation. So they raised the stakes, sometimes hiding when they don't even need to. Today, stardom is more ephemeral and it's photography that gives them their celebrity status."
Ron Galella (1931), American photographer

"I still think photographers should be lashed out at. They should be put in a cage where you can poke them with a stick for a quarter. But not in a hostile way, just for giggles. They really are on the attack against mankind; it's a disease. They should be helped somewhere. But I'd still like to poke them with a stick."
Sean Penn (1960), American actor

"I feel I have an unspoken deal with the paparazzi: 'I won't do anything publicly interesting if you agree not to follow me.'"
Matt Damon (1970), American actor

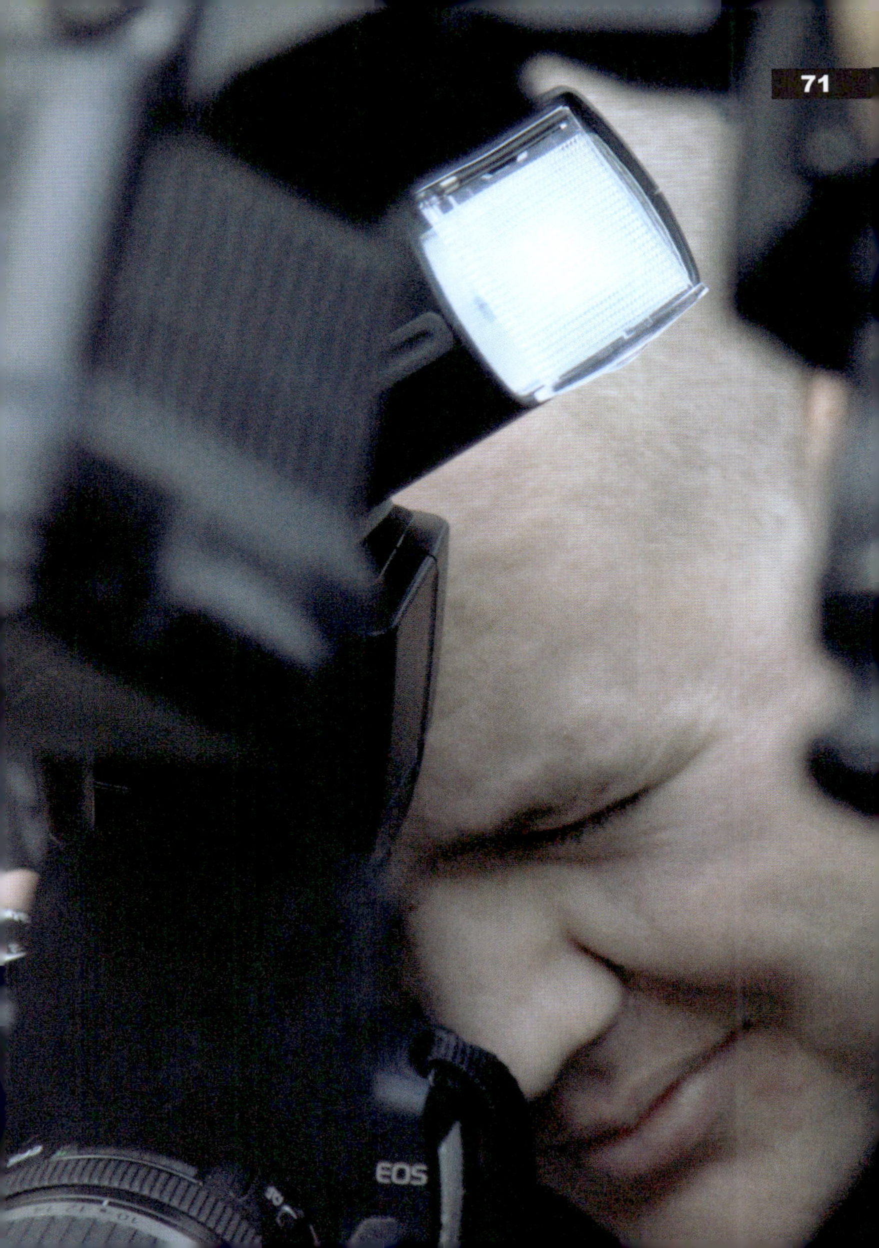

Keep door closed!

In this digital day and age, the darkroom – with its developing baths, processing chemicals, light-sensitive paper and intimidating door signs – seems a relic of the past. With photographers coming out of their darkroom and turning their attention to digital imaging, the risk of ruining a perfectly good roll of film due to light exposure is gone altogether. Alas, in turn the number of photographers who can develop their own film and create and enhance their own prints is dwindling fast.

———

"It is seldom indeed that a composition which was poor when the picture was taken can be improved by reshaping it in the darkroom."
Henri Cartier-Bresson (1908-2004), French photographer

"When I go into the darkroom, I'm totally in my own territory... I need nothing in that darkroom but the opportunity to drop a few sheets of paper in the developer and listen to classical music, and I feel as if I've levitated myself away from all the evils of the world."
Don McCullin (1935), British photographer

"A photographer needs to be a good editor of negatives and prints! In fact, most of the prints I make are for my eyes only, and they are no good. I find the single most valuable tool in the darkroom is my trash can - that's where most of my prints end up."
John Sexton (1953), American photographer

"To convey in the print the feeling you experienced when you exposed your film - to walk out of the darkroom and say: 'This is it, the equivalent of what I saw and felt!' That's what it's all about."
John Sexton (1953), American photographer

Develop an eye

rule 28

Can you learn to look at life through a lens? It's a question that has preoccupied those interested in photography since the early days of the medium. Some believe that you're simply born with a so-called photographer's eye. Others insist that it's possible to develop and train one's photographic vision. Whether or not the photographic eye is indeed a matter of nature or nurture remains subject to debate. A debate that over the years has resulted in some great one-liners, some of which are posted here.

———

"The important thing is not the camera but the eye."
Alfred Eisenstaedt (1898-1995),
German-born American photographer

"It's not what you look at that matters, it's what you see."
Henry David Thoreau (1817-1862),
American writer and philosopher

"A photographer's main instrument is his eyes. Strange as it may seem, many photographers choose to use the eyes of another photographer, past or present, instead of their own. Those photographers are blind."
Manuel Alvarez Bravo (1902-2002),
Mexican photographer

"Stare. It is the way to educate your eye…"
Walker Evans (1903-1975), American photographer

"The camera doesn't make a bit of difference. All of them can record what you are seeing. But, you have to SEE."
Ernst Haas (1921-1986), Austrian photographer

"Insofar as the photographic frame, let us say that being a photographer entails 'having an eye'. It can't be learnt - at best, you can only learn a few 'tricks'."
Yann Arthus-Bertrand (1946), French photographer

"I usually have in my mind what everything is, which can also be very difficult. You have to explain it to many people many times, and still when I get there it's usually not the way I want it. I am asking people to interpret and it's not easy. They don't have the same eye as me."
Steven Meisel (1954), American photographer

"For me, the most important thing I learned was just honing my eye. I think I had a good eye."
Herb Ritts (1952-2002), American photographer

"It's my decision, it's my eye. The photographer has the biggest influence on the picture."
Viviane Sassen (1972), Dutch photographer

"Remember, not everything is a picture. A good eye can edit before the shutter opens."
Craig Coverdale, Australian street photographer

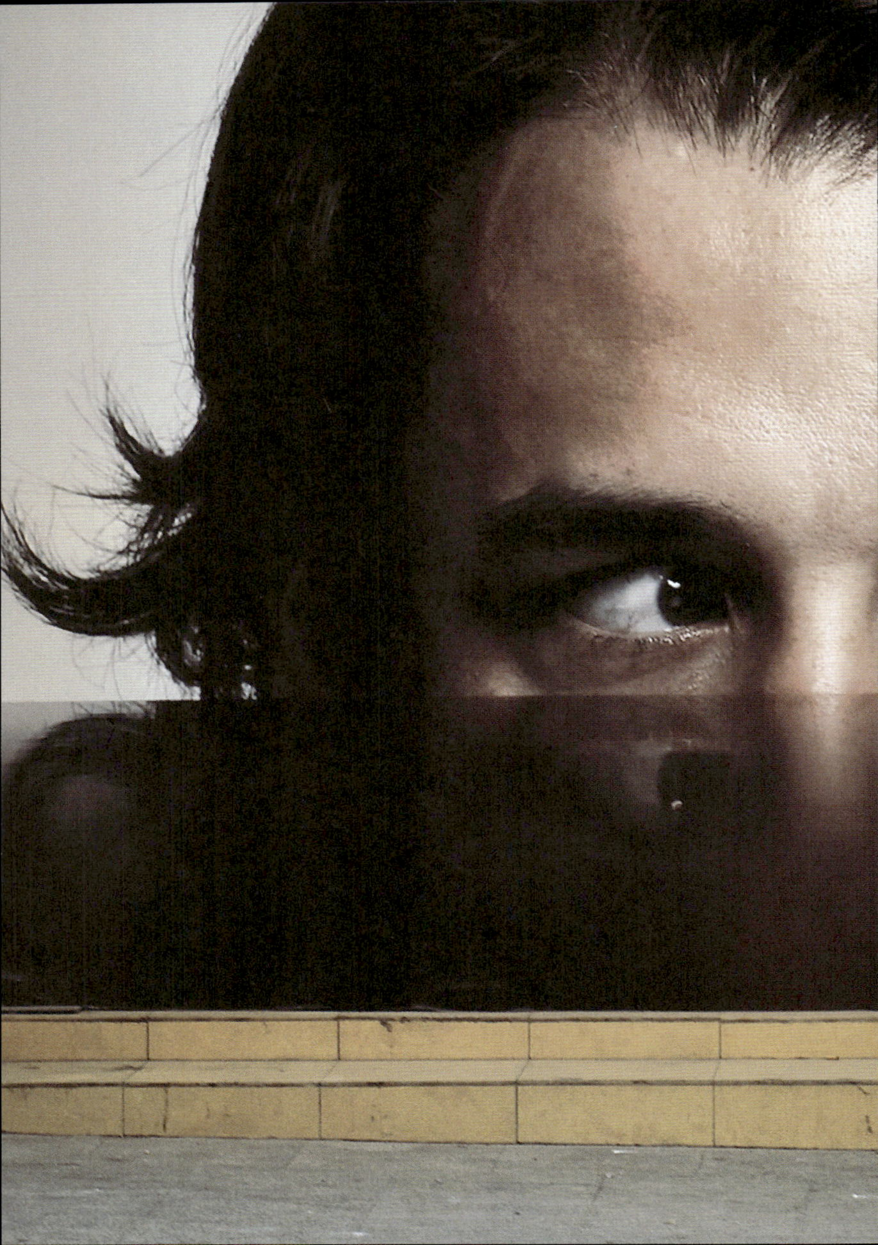

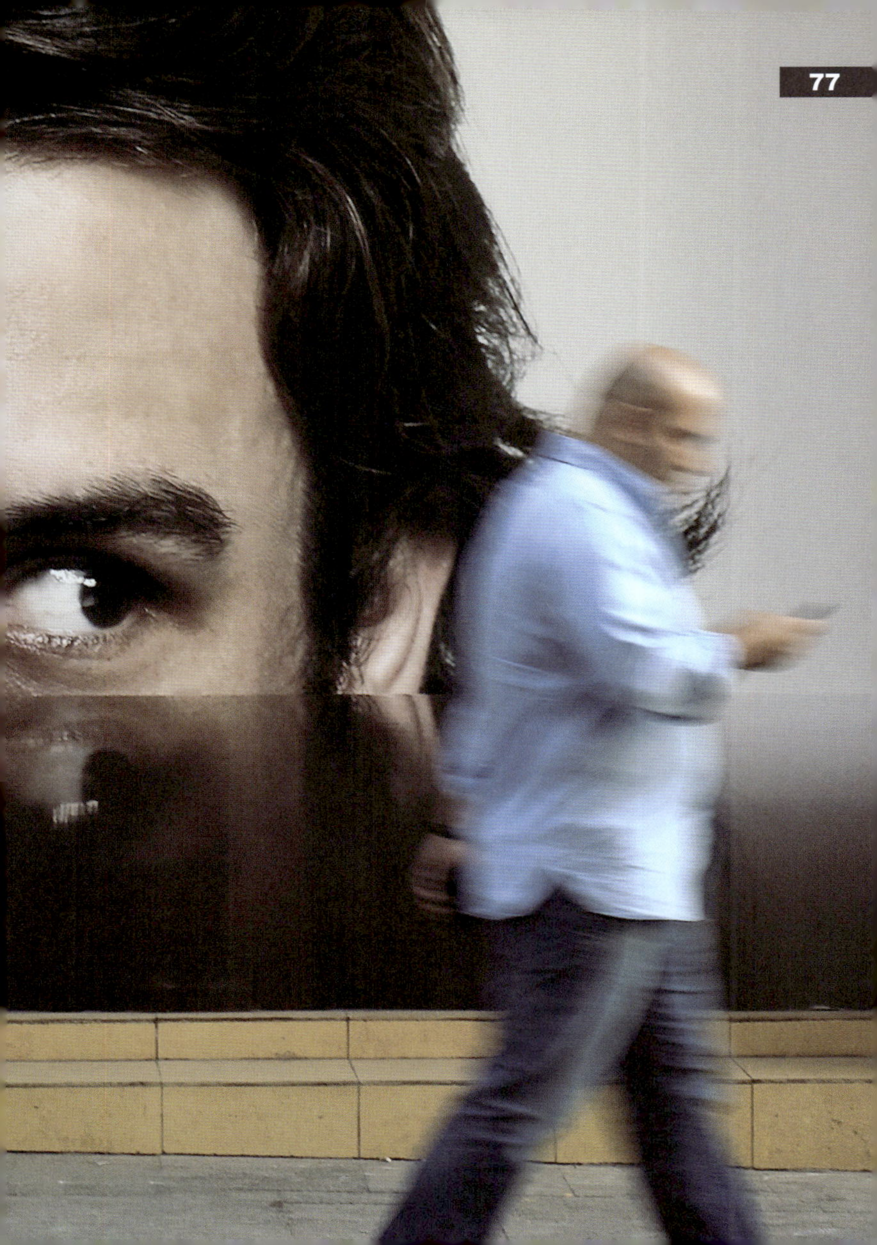

All photographers are voyeurs

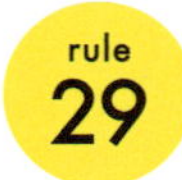

To quote the enigmatic fashion photographer Helmut Newton (1920-2004): "Any photographer who says he's not a voyeur is either stupid or a liar."

"We photographers are nothing but a pack of crooks, thieves and voyeurs. We are to be found everywhere we are not wanted; we betray secrets that were never entrusted to us; we spy shamelessly on things that are not our business; and end up the hoarders of a vast quantity of stolen goods."
George Brassaï (1899-1984), Hungarian photographer

"I always thought of photography as a naughty thing to do - that was one of my favorite things about it, and when I first did it, I felt very perverse."
Diane Arbus (1923-1971), American photographer

"There is a popular notion that the photographer is by nature a voyeur, the last one to be invited to the party. But I'm not crashing; this is my party. This is my family, my friends."
Nan Goldin (1953), American photographer

"I am not a voyeur, as voyeurs photograph through closed windows and with me the window is always wide open."
Nan Goldin (1953), American photographer

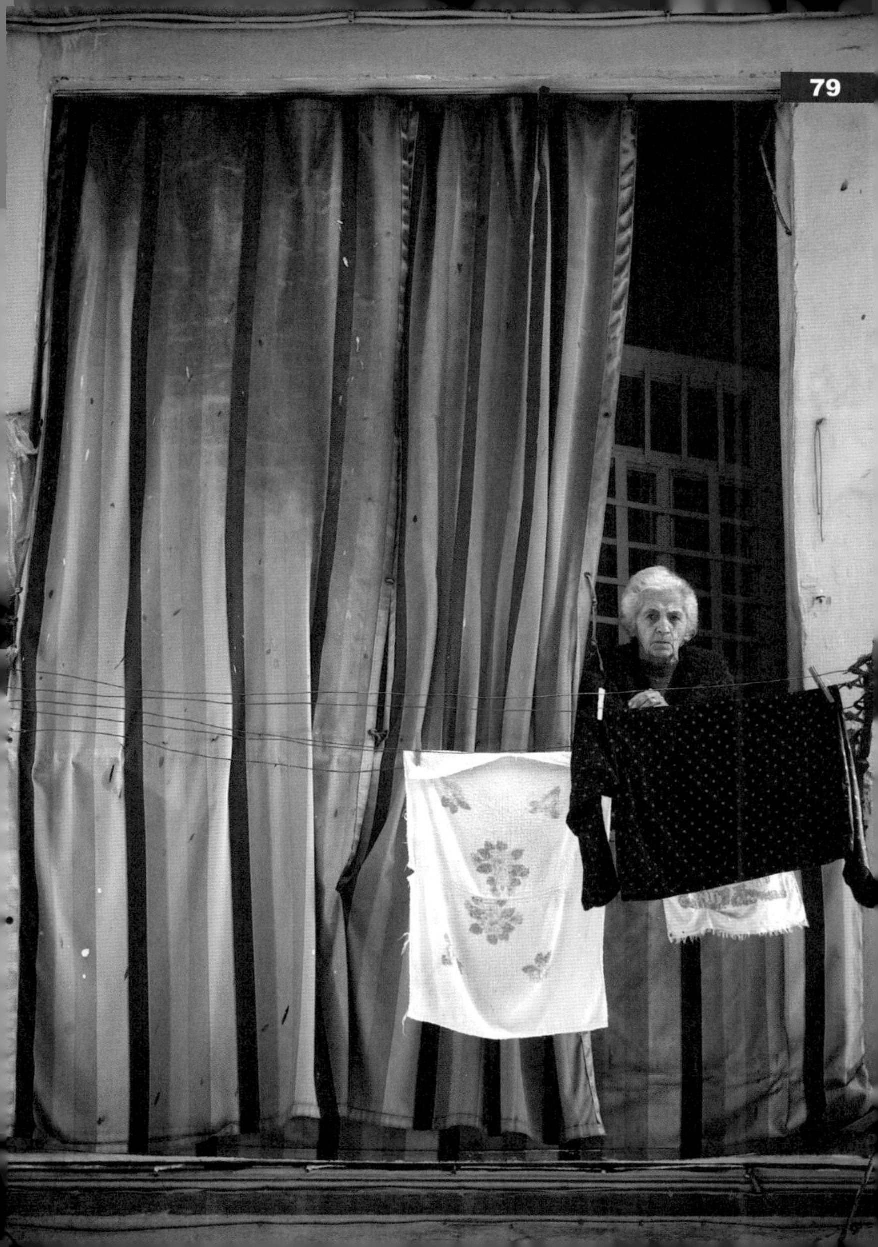

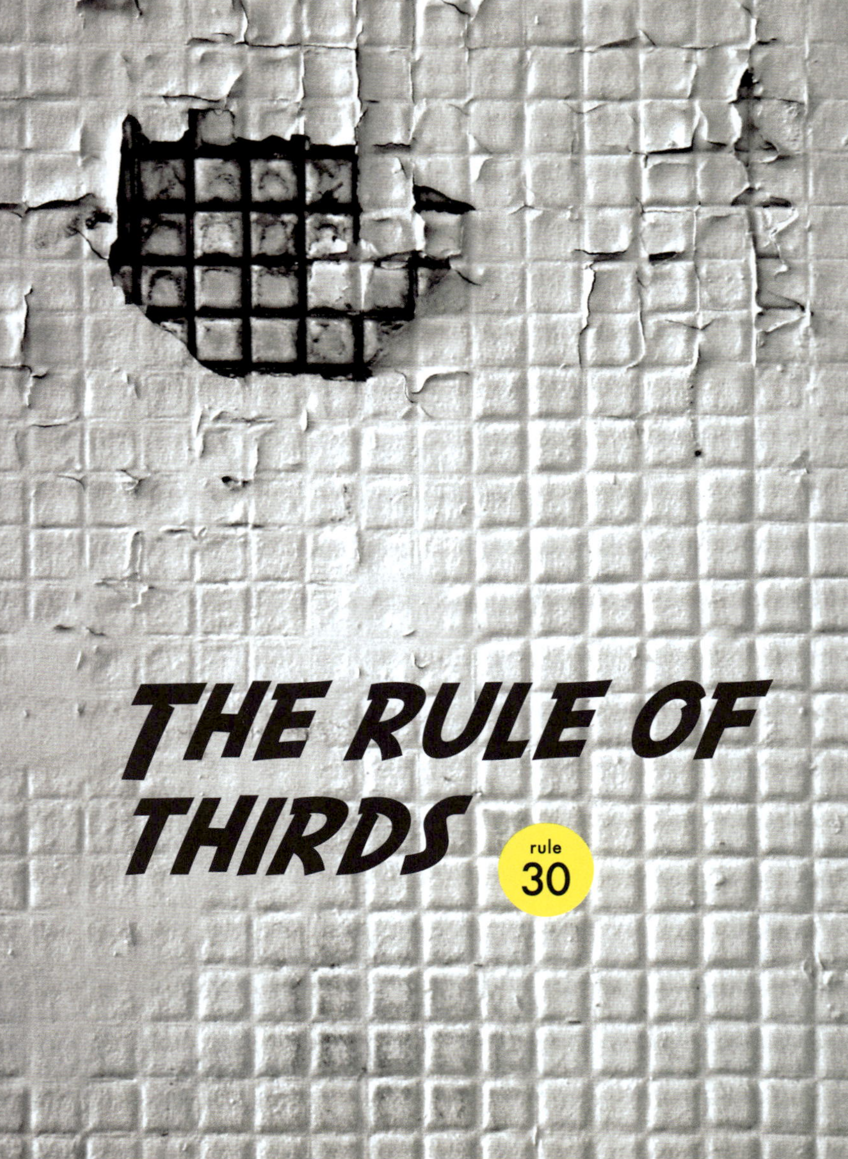

THE RULE OF THIRDS
rule
30

This composition guideline has helped many a painter, (graphic) designer and indeed photographer to create more dynamic, balanced and aesthetically-pleasing work. The rule calls for a 9-panel grid to be placed over the scene or shot that is created. Things that are of visual importance are ideally placed where the vertical and horizontal lines intersect. The rule first seems to pop up in 'Remarks on Rural Scenery' by British painter and engraver John Thomas Smith back in 1797. The rule of thirds remains an important guideline in photography although it has always had stiff competition of the golden mean, which some believe to be a better compositional guideline.

———————

"I have presumed to think that, in connecting or in breaking the various lines of a picture, it would likewise be a good rule to do it, in general, by a similar scheme of proportion; for example, in a design of landscape, to determine the sky at about two thirds; or else at about one third, so that the material objects might occupy the other two: Again, two thirds of one element (as of water), to one third of another element (as of land); and then both together to make but one third of the picture, of which the two other thirds should go for the sky and aerial perspectives. This rule would likewise apply in breaking a length of wall, or any other too great continuation of line that it may be found necessary to break by crossing or hiding it with some other object: In short, in applying this invention, generally speaking, or to any other case, whether of light, shade, form, or color, I have found the ratio of about two thirds to one third, or of one to two, a much better and more harmonizing proportion, than the precise formal half, the two-far-extending four fifths—and, in short, than any other proportion whatsoever."
John Thomas Smith (1766–1833), British painter and engraver

"To consult the rules of composition before making a picture is a little like consulting the law of gravitation before going for a walk."
Edward Weston (1886-1958), American photographer

TAKE YOUR TIME

The element of time has an important part to play in photography. As a photographer you're forever capturing moments in time. But taking time also means putting in the hours, shooting image after image, sometimes for years on end, in an effort to hone your photographic skills. Don't expect to produce a great shot overnight. Indeed, as French photographer Henri Cartier-Bresson (1908-2004) aptly pointed out: "Your first 10,000 photographs are your worst." Give it time.

———

"A photographer is like a cod, which produces a million eggs in order that one may reach maturity."
George Bernard Shaw (1856-1950), Irish playwright

"There is no such thing as taking too much time, because your soul is in that picture."
Ruth Bernhard (1905-2006), German-born American photographer

"Think about the photo before and after, never during. The secret is to take your time. You mustn't go too fast. The subject must forget about you. Then, however, you must be very quick. So, if you miss the picture, you've missed it. So what?"
Henri Cartier-Bresson (1908-2004), French photographer

"Give it all you got for at least 5 years and then decide if you got what it takes. Too many great talents give up at the very beginning; the great black hole looming after the comfortable academy or university years is the number one killer of future talent."
Carl De Keyzer (1958), Belgian photographer

"Stick to one project for a long time. And keep working on it through many stages of learning, even if it might feel finished. It's the only way to break through what I think are some vital lessons that need to be learnt about story-telling and how to combine images."
Mikhael Subotzky (1981), South African photographer

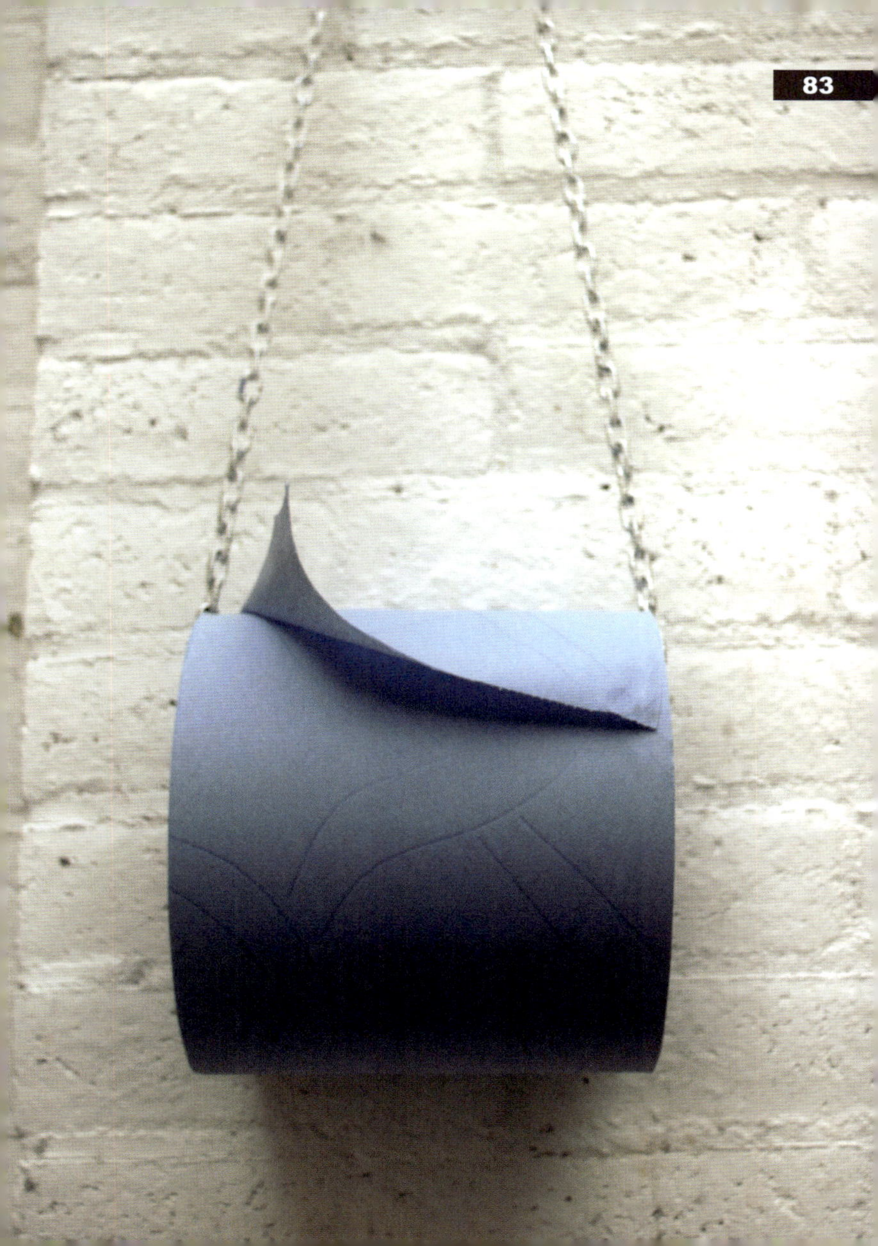

Seize the moment

rule 32

The list of quotes and one-liners by French photographer Henri Cartier-Bresson (1908-2004) on the fleeting nature of photography is endless. Hardly surprising, given the fact that he authored 'The Decisive Moment', a photographic classic from 1952. According to Bresson, photographers are "always struggling with time," and he adds that "whatever has gone, has gone forever. The time element is the key to photography. One must seize the moment before it passes, the fleeting gesture, the evanescent smile."

———

"Photography to me is catching a moment which is passing, and which is true."
Jacques-Henri Lartigue (1894-1986), French photographer and painter

"You know there are moments such as these when time stands still and all you do is hold your breath and hope it will wait for you. And you just hope you will have time enough to get it organized in a fraction of a second on that tiny piece of sensitive film."
Dorothea Lange (1895-1965), American photographer

"Life is very fluid. Sometimes the pictures disappear and there's nothing you can do. You can't tell the person, 'Oh, please smile again. Do that gesture again.' Life is once, forever."
Henri Cartier-Bresson (1908-2004), French photographer

"What I like about photographs is that they capture a moment that's gone forever, impossible to reproduce."
Karl Lagerfeld (1938), German fashion designer

"Photography is about a single point of a moment. It's like stopping time. As everything gets condensed in that forced instant. But if you keep creating these points, they form a line which reflects your life."
Nobuyoshi Araki (1940), Japanese photographer

"I'm into capturing the moment. Sometimes, I'll rip the camera out of my assistant's hands and he'll be shouting, 'But there's no film in the camera!' and I think, 'Never mind! Let's go.'"
Ellen von Unwerth (1954), German photographer

CONSIDER A TRIPOD

There's a certain charm to shooting from the hip, but if it's steady shots and free hands you're after the three-legged tripod comes in handy. For as British photographer Lawrence Sackmann aptly pointed out "your tripod and your camera must be well-fixed but your eyes and mind should be free."

———————

"In my work, the most elaborate – and essential – accessory is a standard tripod. For spiritual companions I have had the many artists who have relied on nature to help shape their imagination. And their most elaborate equipment was a deep reverence for the world through which they passed. Photographers share something with these artists. We seek only to see and to describe with our own voices, and, though we are seldom heard as soloists, we cannot photograph the world in any other way."
Sam Abell (1945), American photographer

"I like to be flexible in the way I take pictures. I do not use a tripod, and I move around in the crowd, of which I myself am part... I try to preserve the dynamics of the street, and my way of using the camera tries to approximate as much as possible the way we see: focusing on details, opening up to wider angles, and composing all these very short, fragmented impressions into a larger mental picture."
Beat Streuli (1957), Swiss photographer and artist

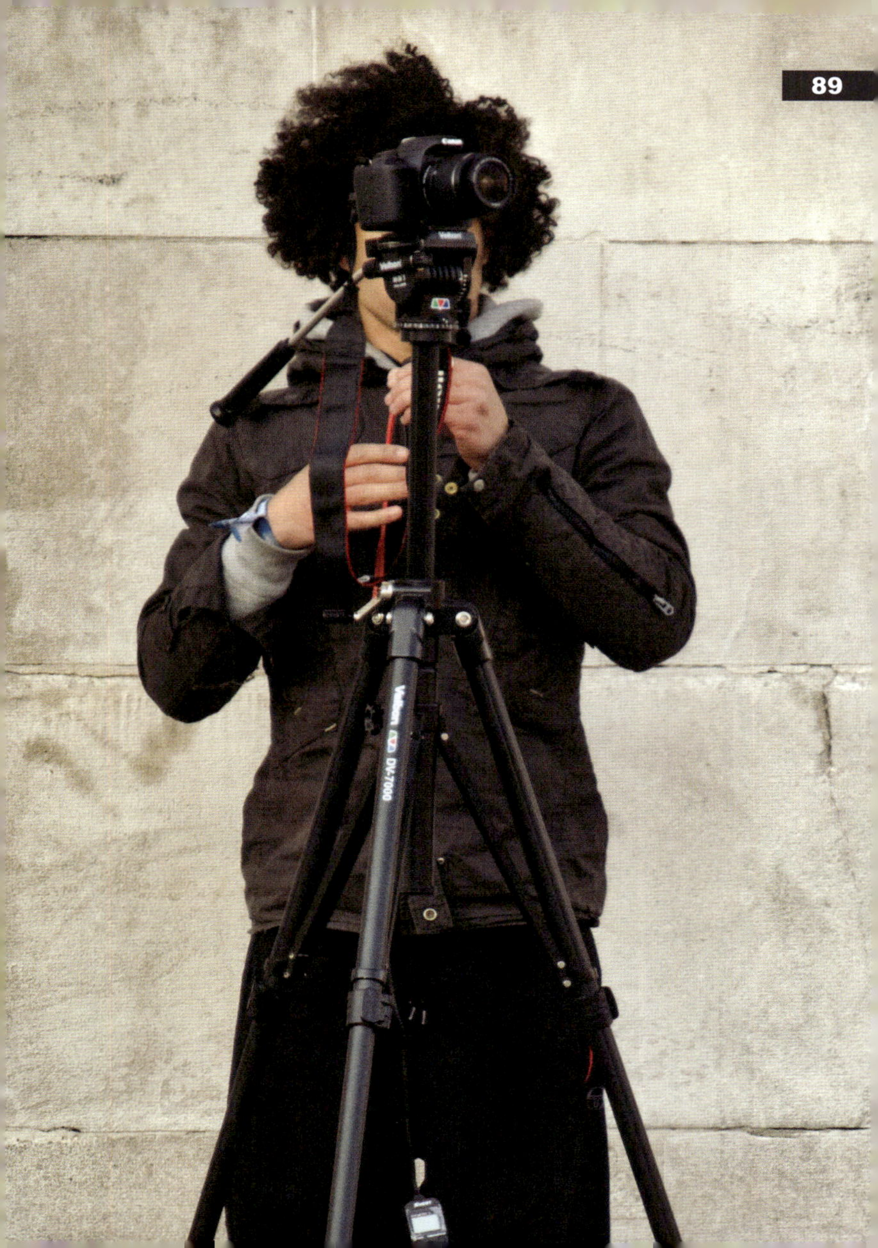

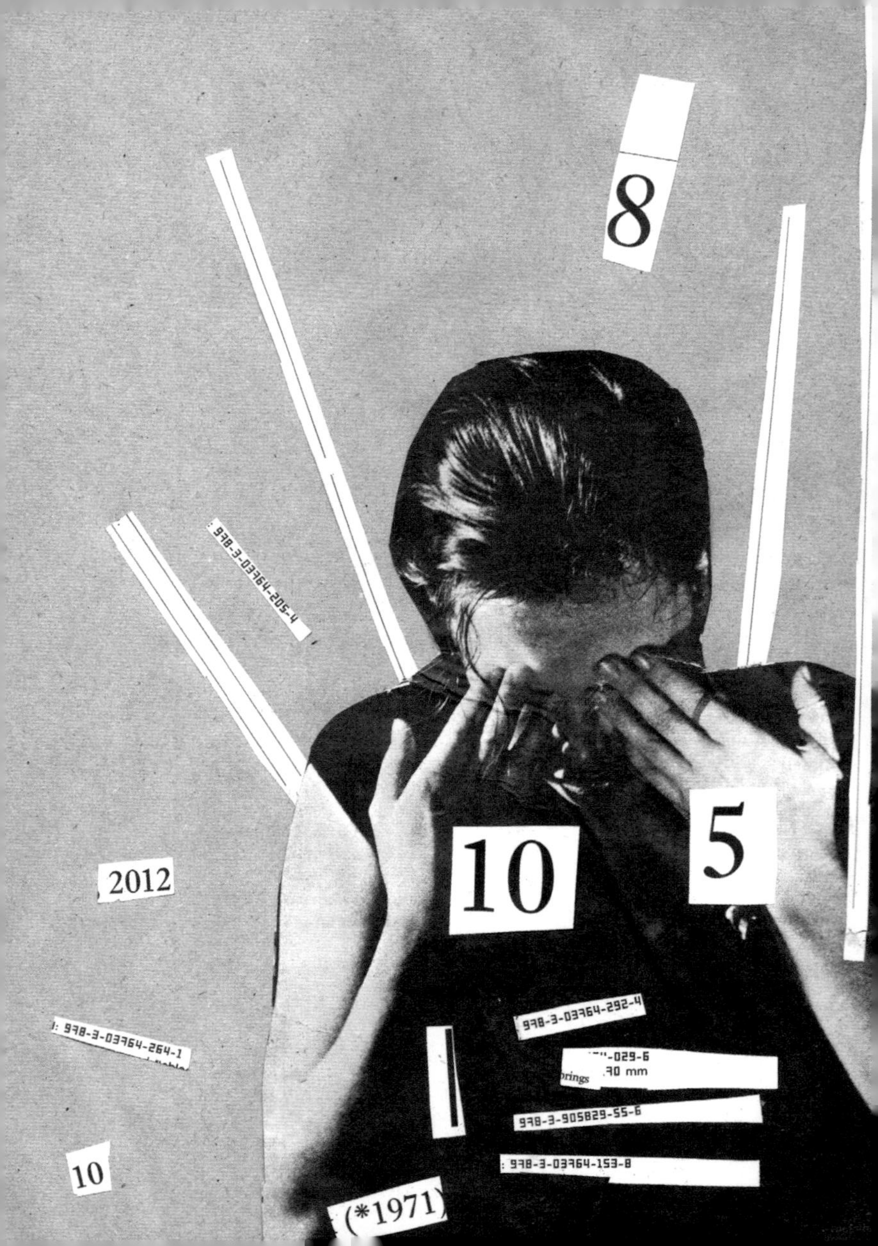

8

2012

978-3-03764-205-4

978-3-03764-264-1

10

10

5

978-3-03764-292-4

029-6
.70 mm
brings

978-3-905829-55-6

978-3-03764-153-8

(*1971)

KEEP IT SIMPLE, STUPID

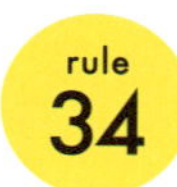

"Keep It Simple, Stupid." "Keep It Small and Scalable." "Keep It Short and Simple." "Keep It Sweet and Simple." The well-known K.I.S.S. rule is used in the worlds of design, advertising, fashion, typography and plenty of other creative fields, including the world of photography.

"It is by great economy of means that one arrives at simplicity of expression."
Henri Cartier-Bresson (1908-2004), French photographer

"What's really important is to simplify. The work of most photographers would be improved immensely if they could do one thing: get rid of the extraneous. If you strive for simplicity, you are more likely to reach the viewer."
William Albert Allard (1937), American photographer

"In photography, the two words I like most are 'simplicity' and 'authenticity'. I try to see things with authenticity, in natural manner: no cheating in order to show things as they are. This is the way in which I would like to see things. My ideal point of view."
Yann Arthus-Bertrand (1946), French photographer

"You limit your choices from the beginning. So I don't bring a lot of lenses, cameras, all these elements that can help the picture. You confine yourself to, say, one room and you just make it work. You become very creative in that little space. You have left a lot of other options out of the game."
Anton Corbijn (1955), Dutch photographer

Photography isn't art

It took photography a mighty long time to claim its rightful place in the world of art. And even today there's discussion about whether or not photography is indeed an art form or something that on occasion can produce works of art. The role of the photographer seems to be the decisive factor in the whole debate. To some a photographer is nothing more than a technician that operates what is in essence a recording medium to reproduce an image of something that is already there. This rather narrow definition does not do justice to the active and indeed creative role that photographers play. After all, they play with light and composition in creating an image, just like centuries of painters have done before them.

"The limitations of photography are so great that, though the results may, and sometimes do give a certain aesthetic pleasure, the medium must rank the lowest of all arts, lower than any graphic art, for the individuality of the artist is cramped, in short, it can hardly show itself."
Peter Henry Emerson (1856-1936), British writer and photographer

"Is photography an art? There is no point in trying to find out if it is an art. Art is old-fashioned. We need something else."
Man Ray (1890-1976), American artist

"It is easy to take a photograph, but it is harder to make a masterpiece in photography than in any other art medium."
Ansel Adams (1902-1984), American photographer

"The word 'art' is very slippery. It really has no importance in relation to one's work. I work for the pleasure, for the pleasure of the work, and everything else is a matter for the critics."
Manuel Álvarez Bravo (1902-2002), Mexican photographer

"Photography is not like painting. There is a creative fraction of a second when you are taking a picture. Your eye must see a composition or an expression that life itself offers you, and you must know with intuition when to click the camera. That is the moment the photographer is creative."
Henri Cartier-Bresson (1908-2004), French photographer

"Some people's photography is an art. Not mine. Art is a dirty word in photography. All this fine art crap is killing it already."
Helmut Newton (1920-2004), German-Australian photographer

"Photography has always reminded me of the second child, trying to prove itself. The fact that it wasn't really considered an art... that it was considered a craft... has trapped almost every serious photographer."
Richard Avedon (1923-2004), American photographer

"Time eventually positions most photographs, even the most amateurish, at the level of art."
Susan Sontag (1933-2004), American writer and filmmaker

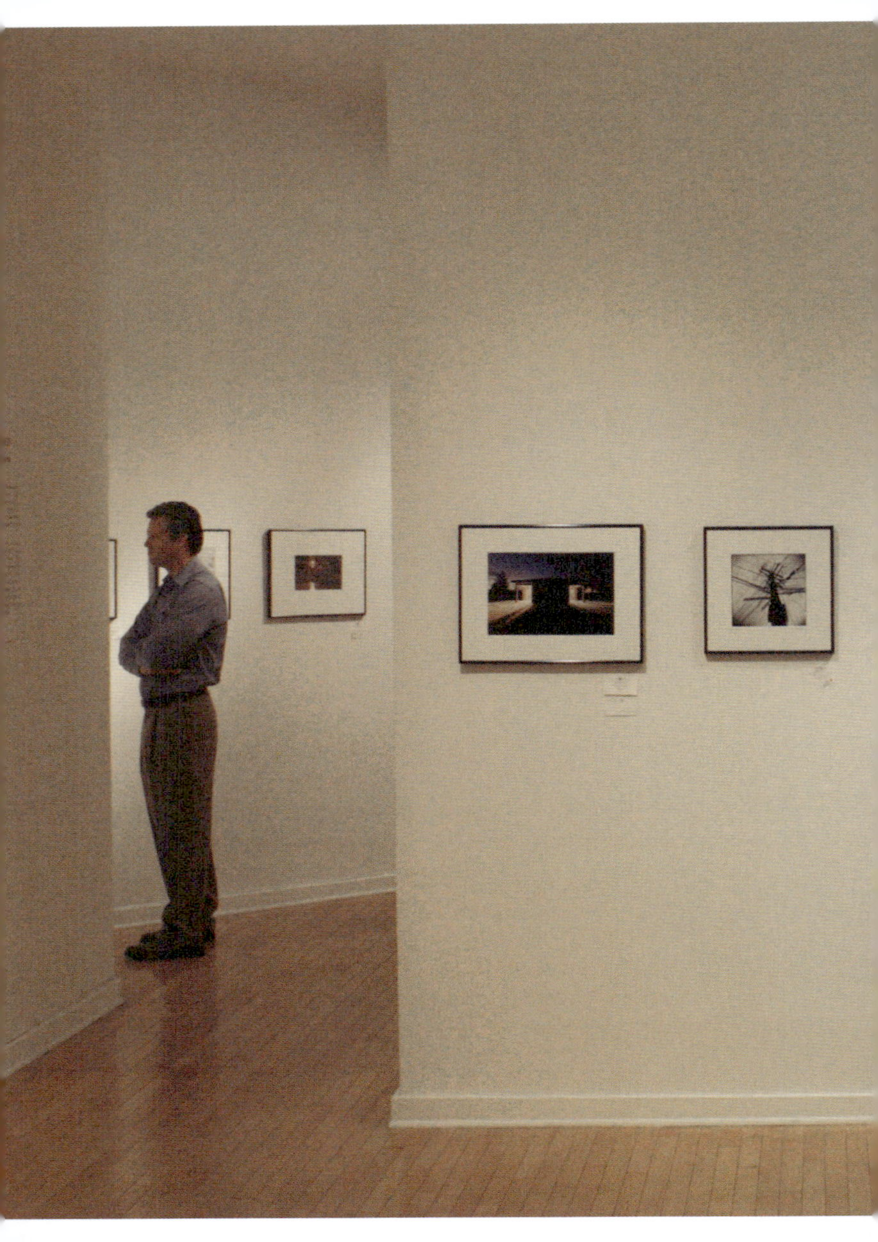

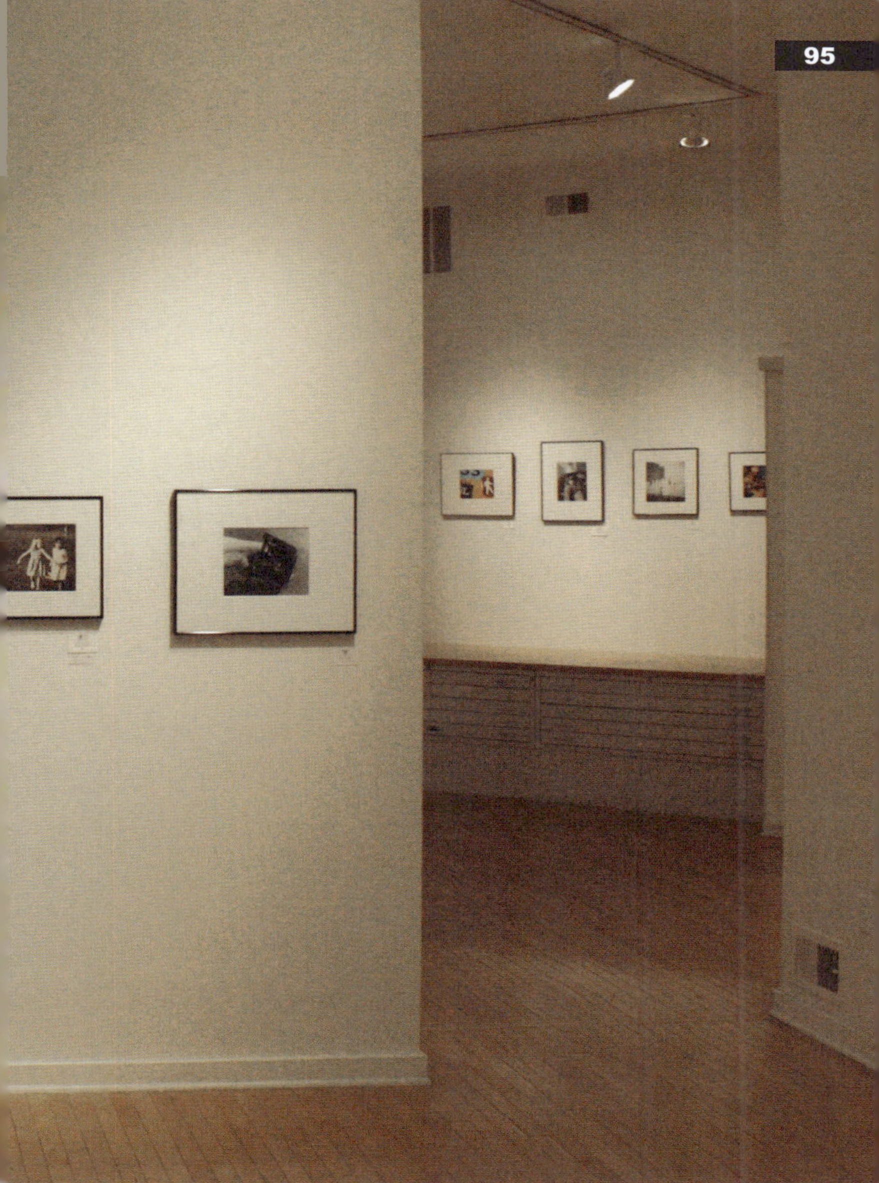

"A portrait is not a likeness."

Best known for his black-and-white celebrity portraits and fashion photography, Richard Avedon (1923 – 2004) has been hailed as the master of portrait photography. In his sixty-year career he captured Hollywood legends such as Marilyn Monroe and Audrey Hepburn, musical geniuses such as Janis Joplin and Bob Dylan, as well as (former) American presidents, including Dwight Eisenhower and John F. Kennedy. With such an impressive career and portfolio, who'd dare to disagree with Avedon's claim that "a portrait is not a likeness"?

"The most difficult thing for me is a portrait. You have to try and put your camera between the skin of a person and his shirt."
Henri Cartier-Bresson (1908-2004), French photographer

"My photographs do me an injustice. They look just like me."
Phyllis Diller (1917), American comedienne

"A portrait is not a likeness. The moment an emotion or fact is transformed into a photograph it is no longer a fact but an opinion."
Richard Avedon (1923-2004), American photographer

"In a portrait, you have room to have a point of view. The image may not be literally what's going on, but it's representative."
Annie Leibovitz (1949), American photographer

"You hope to get something from the person you photograph that's different than other images you know of these people."
Anton Corbijn (1955), Dutch photographer

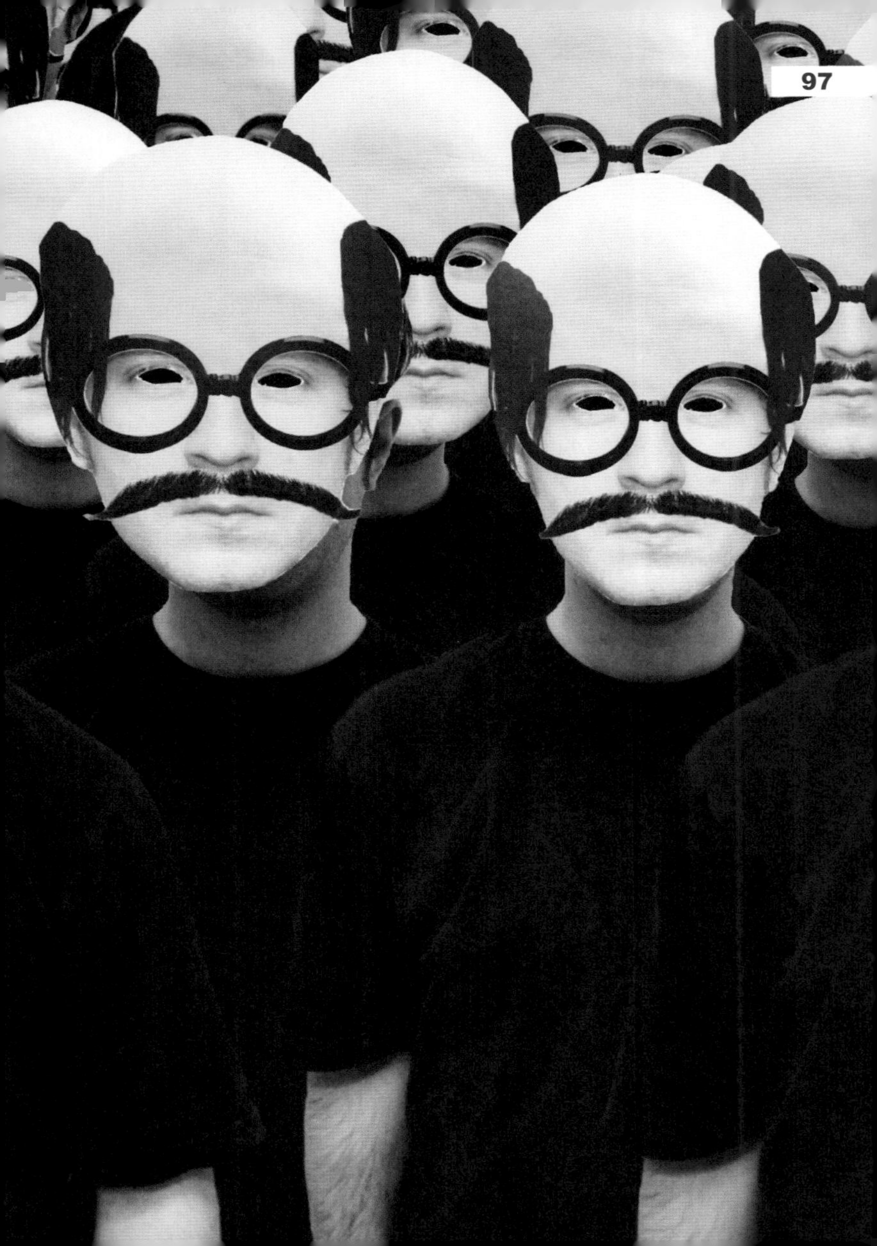

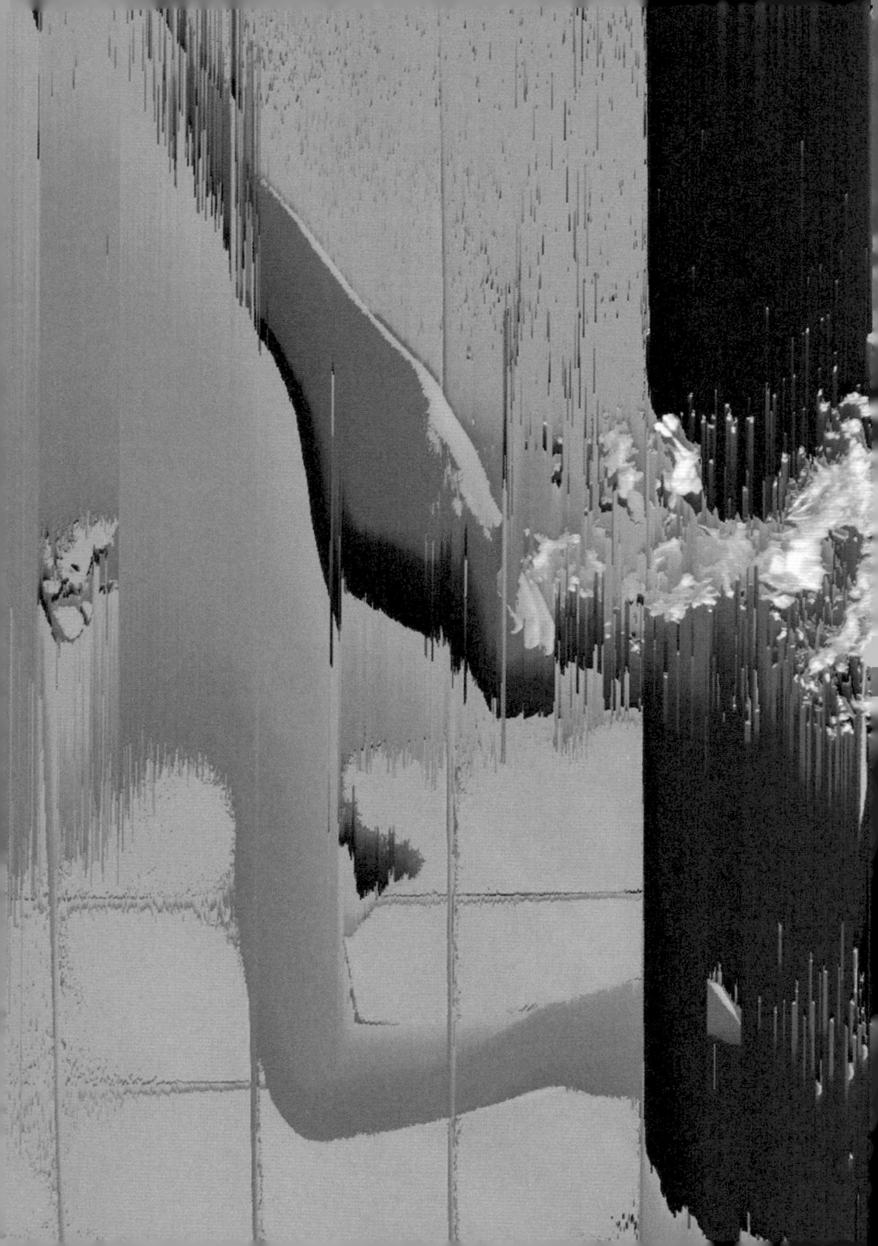

FREEZE THE ACTION

• • • • •

SHOW THE MOTION

If you want to capture movement or action in still photography you can either opt to freeze the action or show the motion. The first requires a fast shutter speed and results in images that are blur-free but also devoid of any action. A lower shutter speed results in images that might have more blur but also more action, showing motion.

"A shutter working at a speed of one-fourth to one-twenty-fifth of a second will answer all purposes. A little blur in a moving subject will often aid to giving the impression of action and motion."
Alfred Stieglitz (1864-1946),
American photographer

Learn the craft

rule 39

Photography is as much an art as it is a craft. And while it seems a bit of a no-brainer, it's important to learn your craft. Get to know the equipment you work with. Look at the work of others. Pick up a book. Watch a good documentary. Take a class. Anything to hone your craft.

———————

"Learn the craft (which is not very hard). Carefully study past work of photographers and classic painters. Look at and learn from movies. See where you can fit in as a 'commercial' photographer. Commercial, meaning working for others and delivering a product on command. But most of all, keep your personal photography as your separate hobby. If you are very good and diligent, it just may pay off."
Elliott Erwitt (1928), French-born American photographer

"Learn from the best; the second-raters have nothing to offer."
David Hurn (1934), British photographer

"Avoid all photo schools and courses. Most will give you lofty ideas and twist your mind in one direction. Find your own way to photography; nobody will ask you later if you have a diploma. Visit as many museums as you possibly can. The images you see (painted, drawn, etched or photographed) will stay with you for the rest of your life. They will help you to discover good pictures in real life. Suppress any silly ambitions of becoming a great artist. Being a good photographer is difficult enough."
Thomas Hoepker (1936), German photographer

"Study the works of the greatest photographers, like Henri Cartier-Bresson and Andre Kertesz."
Hiroji Kubota (1939), Japanese photographer

"Study photography, see what people have achieved, but learn from it, don't try photographically to be one of those people."
Chris Steele-Perkins (1947), British photographer

"When you start out, you're not really aware. I didn't have a sense of photographic history."
Herb Ritts (1952-2002), American photographer

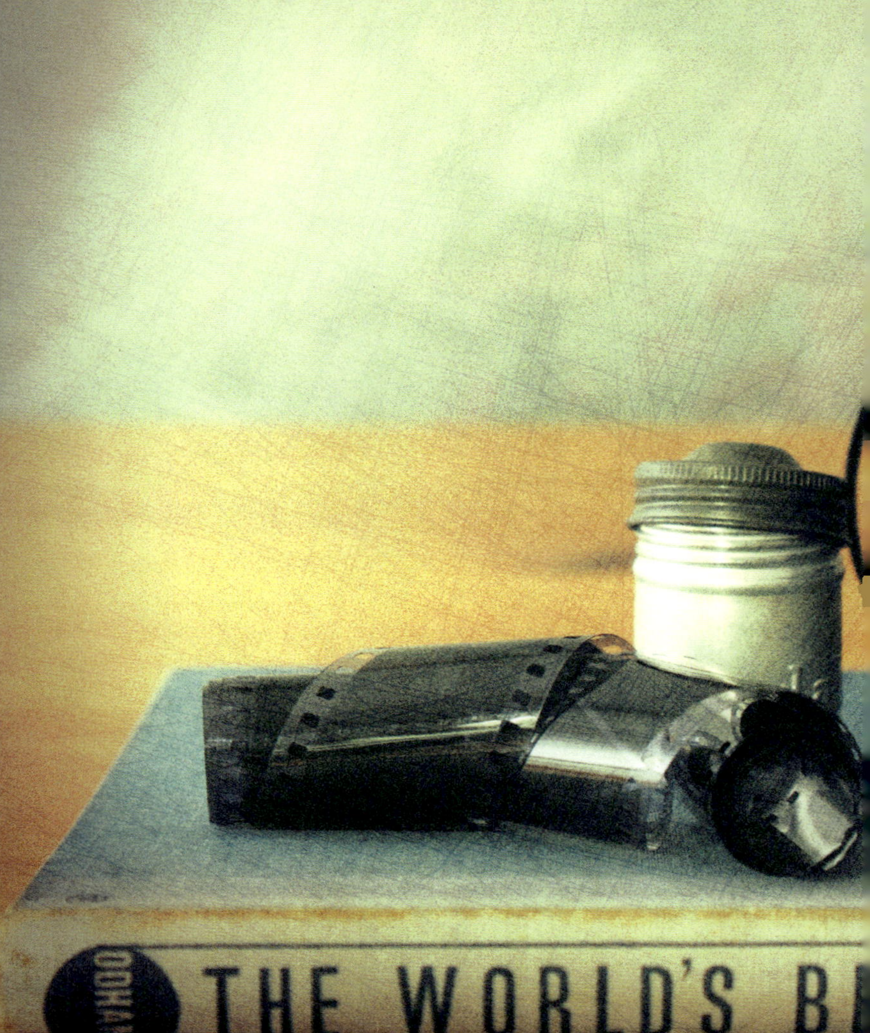

THE WORLD'S B

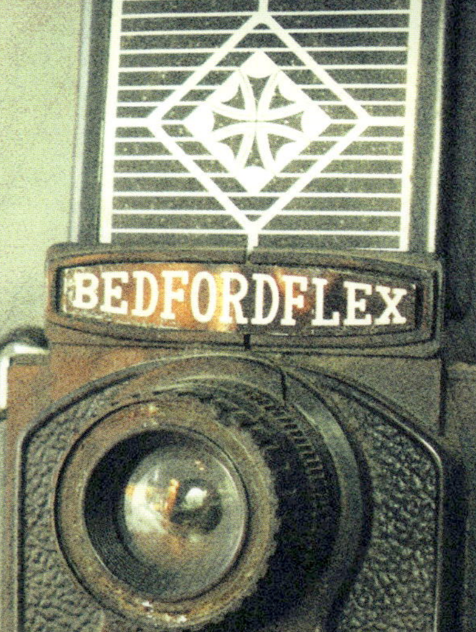
BEDFORDFLEX
f8 SPEED 1/50 SEC.
PLASICION LENS

T PHOTOGRAPHS
THIRD
SERIES

THE WORLD IS YOUR STUDIO

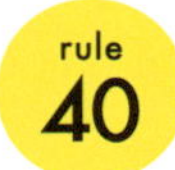

According to Austrian photographer Ernst Haas (1921-1986) there are two kinds of photographers in this world: "Those who compose pictures and those who take them." While the former work in studios, "for the latter, the studio is the world... For them, the ordinary doesn't exist: everything in life is a source of nourishment."

───────

"I always prefer to work in the studio. It isolates people from their environment. They become in a sense… symbolic of themselves."
Richard Avedon (1923-2004), American photographer

"If you are out there shooting, things will happen for you. If you're not out there, you'll only hear about it."
Jay Maisel (1931), American photographer

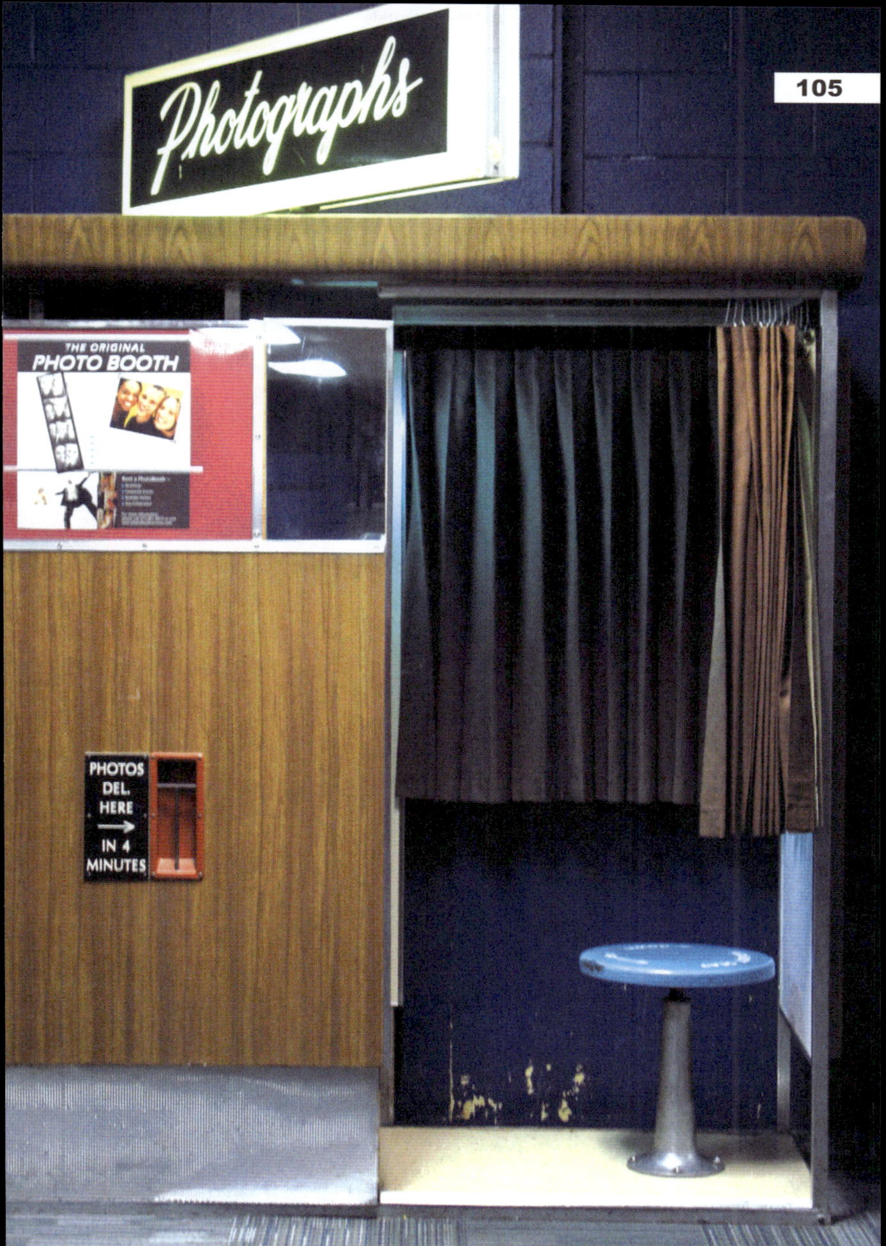

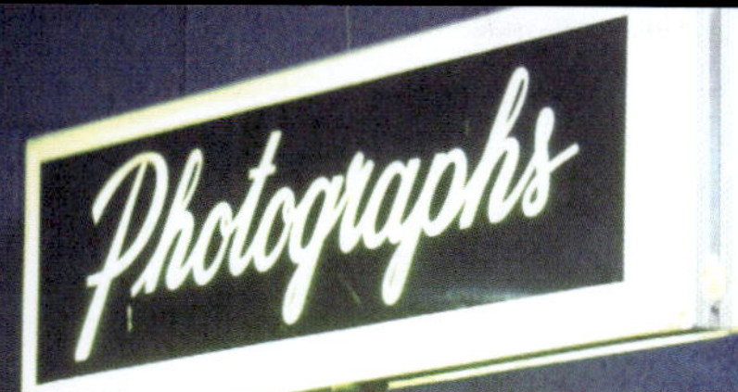
Photographs

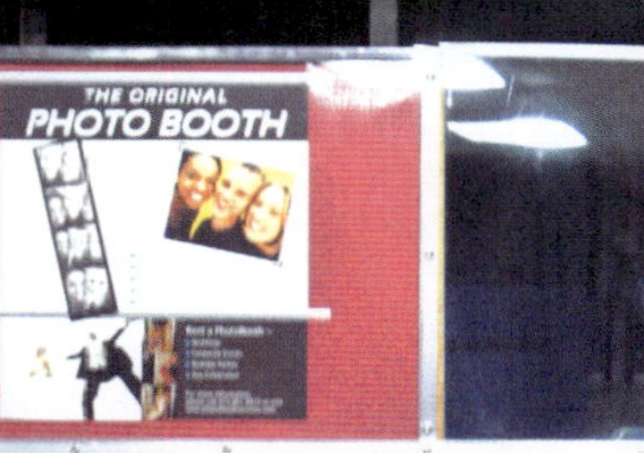
THE ORIGINAL
PHOTO BOOTH

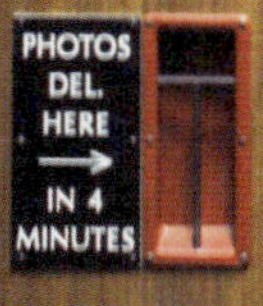
PHOTOS
DEL.
HERE
IN 4
MINUTES

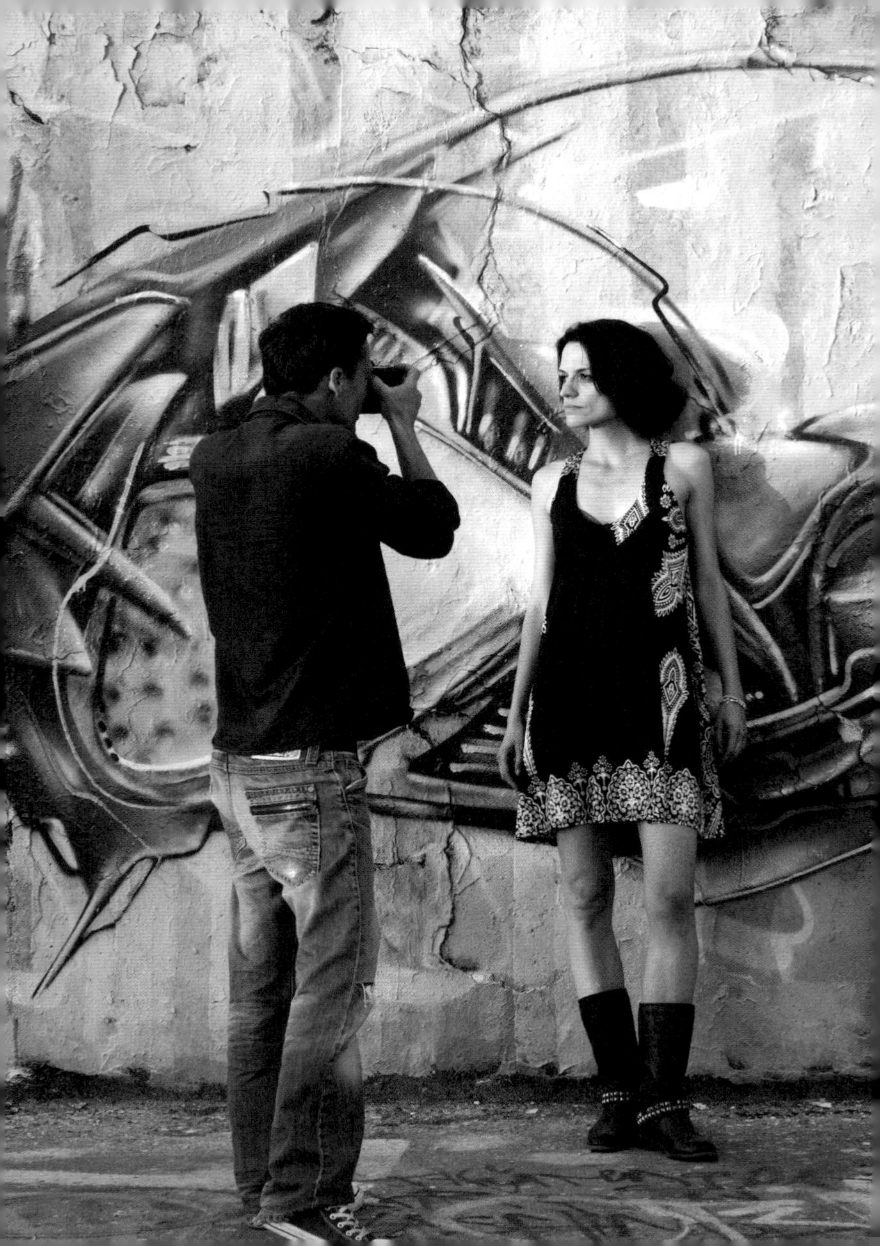

The camera gives confidence

rule 41

It's not just the people that are in front of a camera that get shy. Luckily, the camera often acts as a go-between, a kind of confidence booster that gives even the most timid of photographers the balls to blatantly click away on the streets or tell their model to strike the most trying of poses.

"Many photographers are naturally shy people. Hiding behind a camera helps them overcome their shyness. It's a common experience with photographers that they never notice imminent danger when they've got a camera in their hands. Something sort of takes over."
Thurston Hopkins (1913), British photographer

"Being shy is quite useful to a photographer, because it gives you the opportunity of not being shy once you have the field of a camera before you. It protects you from being shy."
Elliott Erwitt (1928), French-born American photographer

"The problem is, I'm not a good photographer. To be perfectly honest, I'm too shy. Not aggressive enough. Well, I'm not aggressive at all."
Bill Cunningham (1929), American photographer

"'I am a photographer' is an open-sesame to places and people I would otherwise avoid… One of the easiest ways to overcome shyness is to be a photographer."
David Hurn (1934), British photographer

"I was a compulsive shooter… I was very shy, and it was a lot easier for me to communicate if I had a camera between me and other people."
Dennis Hopper (1936-2010), American actor and artist

THE CAMERA WILL STEAL YOUR SOUL

Much has been made of the camera's supposed soul-stealing powers. In the nineteenth century photographers, and their ability to capture people on either a copper plate or a piece of paper with the use of nothing more than a black box, instilled both awe and fear in a public unused to seeing a fixed, lifelike image of themselves. Legend has it that Crazy Horse, the famous Lakota leader, refused to have his picture taken, allegedly stating: "My friend, why should you wish to shorten my life by taking from me my shadow?"

———

"I try to photograph people's spirits and thoughts. As to the soul-taking by the photographer, I don't feel I take away, but rather that the sitter and I give to each other. It becomes an act of mutual participation."
Yousuf Karsh (1908-2002), Canadian photographer

"If each photograph steals a bit of the soul, isn't it possible that I give up pieces of mine every time I take a picture?"
Richard Avedon (1923-2004), American photographer

"People think the camera steals their soul. Places, I am convinced, are affected in the opposite direction. The more they are photographed (or drawn and painted) the more soul they seem to accumulate."
John Pfahl (1939), American photographer

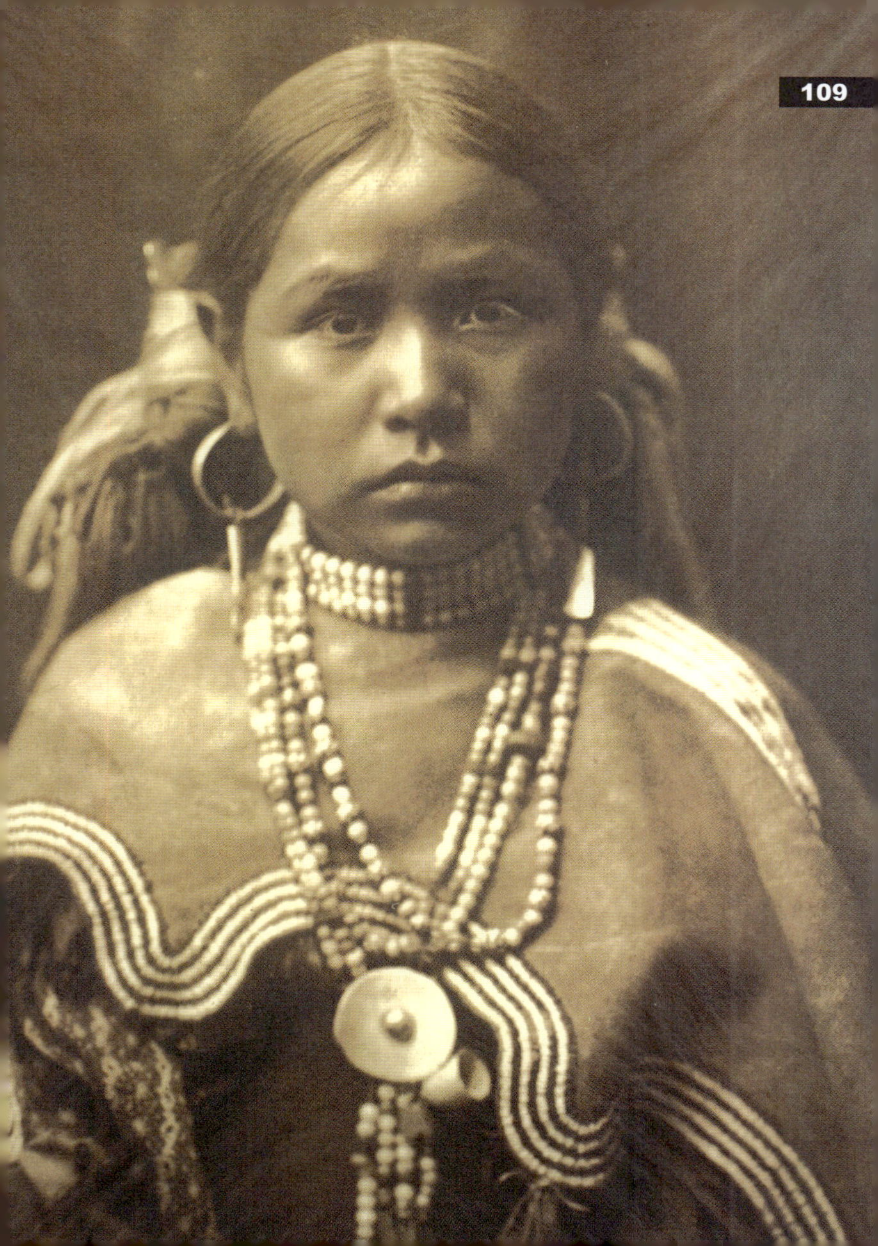

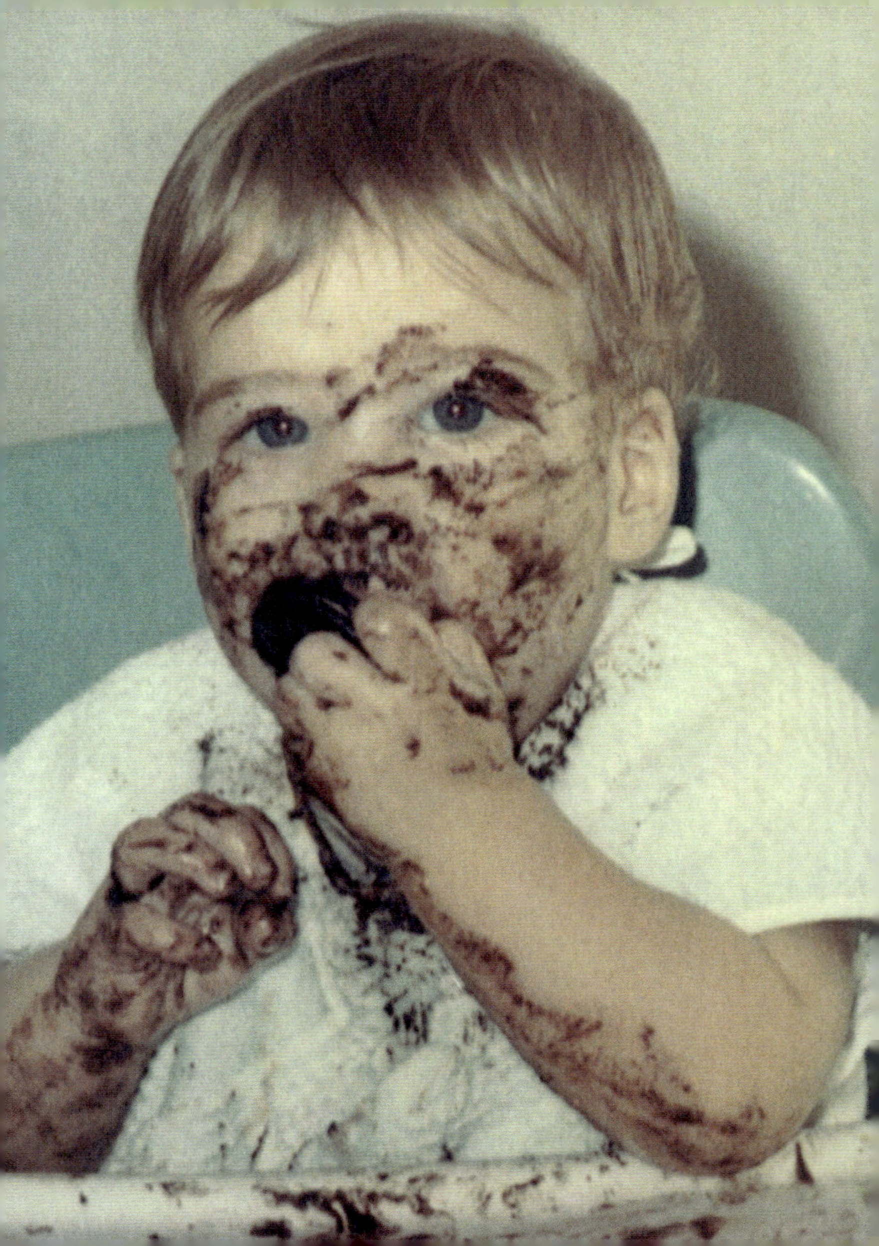

"I just think it's important to be
direct and honest with people about
why you're photographing them and
what you're doing. After all, you are
taking some of their soul."
*Mary Ellen Mark (1940), American
photographer*

"I'm not comfortable having to
be myself or being photographed
as myself. Australian Aborigines
say that with every photo that is
taken, a piece of your soul goes with
it. And there are some days when
I kind of believe that."
*Keira Knightley (1985), British
actress*

"TAKING PICTURES IS LIKE
TIPTOEING INTO THE KITCHEN
LATE AT NIGHT AND STEALING
OREO COOKIES."

Diane Arbus (1923-1971), American photographer

Photoshop is for professionals

First released in 1990 by Adobe, Photoshop was created by the brothers Thomas and John Knoll. Thomas had inherited his father's love for photography, but was also interested in computers. Frustrated by the limitations that came with his newly bought Mac in terms of the manipulation of digital images, Thomas took matters into his own hands and together with his brother ended up creating the well-known image editing program, which introduced the idea of digital photo manipulation to a wider public. Although, in all honesty, as a post-production tool Photoshop is best left to professionals.

"Photoshop is not in my vocabulary. I don't need it because I have content."
Bill Owens (1938), American photographer

"If you want to trick someone with a photograph, there are lots of easy ways to do it. You don't need Photoshop. You don't need sophisticated digital photo-manipulation. You don't need a computer. All you need to do is change the caption."
Errol Morris (1948), American filmmaker

"I know my technique but I'm not too technical, and I really love to just make women look beautiful. I get really excited about it. Instead of doing tons of retouching, I like the challenge of making it happen right then and there."
Ellen von Unwerth (1954), German photographer

"To teach consequential photography, don't bother with Photoshop or f-stops. Create a craving for images."
Douglas McCulloh (1959), American photographer

"The biggest change in my photography has been the introduction of Photoshop and the digital camera. These are the biggest revolutions in the last, well, 20 years."
Erwin Olaf (1959), Dutch photographer

"Lately I've been doing a bit more with the computer, retouching. But most times I never do that. I think that something beautiful is even more charming when it's not too perfect. You don't want to feel the artificiality of the image, you want to believe in it."
Viviane Sassen (1972), Dutch photographer

THE CLIENT IS ALWAYS RIGHT

It may hurt the photographer's artistic heart, or in some cases enormous ego, but the game has changed. The amount of creative freedom available in editorial work has steadily decreased over the years, while the influence of magazine editors, advertising agencies and other clients has only increased. Fighting clients often is futile. Not least because they pay the bills that allow you to embark on more creative personal works. So pick your battles wisely.

———————

"Since the commercialization and banality of editorial magazine pages have made this work uninteresting, advertising has become an increasingly important part of my work. It is interesting to compare European and American mores in regard to my work. One will notice that most of my European images have a stronger sexual content that those destined for American publication. The term 'political correctness' has always appalled me, reminding me of Orwell's 'thought police' and fascist regimes."
Helmut Newton (1920-2004),
German-Australian photographer

"What's more frustrating than magazines giving less and less space is that they tell you what they want. Not LIFE, but some magazines actually want you to be an illustrator, and I don't want to be an illustrator – I don't enjoy those assignments. You know, I want to have a chance to be a real part of the creative process and not just a technician who clicks the camera."
Mary Ellen Mark (1940), American photographer

"Doing editorial work is like being on the road with a band. You don't do your best shit, but you raise the level of your mediocrity and it makes you ready to do your best work when the opportunity comes along."
Robert Polidori (1951), Canadian photographer

"Editorially, there used to be so much freedom that nobody would ask you to shoot a big advertiser for a story. We would, as a joke, put an outfit from Chanel in an editorial, but that was very tongue-in-cheek. Now, basically all the editorial pages are infused by the advertisers."
Inez van Lamsweerde (1963) & Vinoodh Matadin (1961), Dutch photography duo

"Mainstream magazines are more interested in pleasing their clients and thereby allow for much less artistic freedom."
Viviane Sassen (1972), Dutch photographer

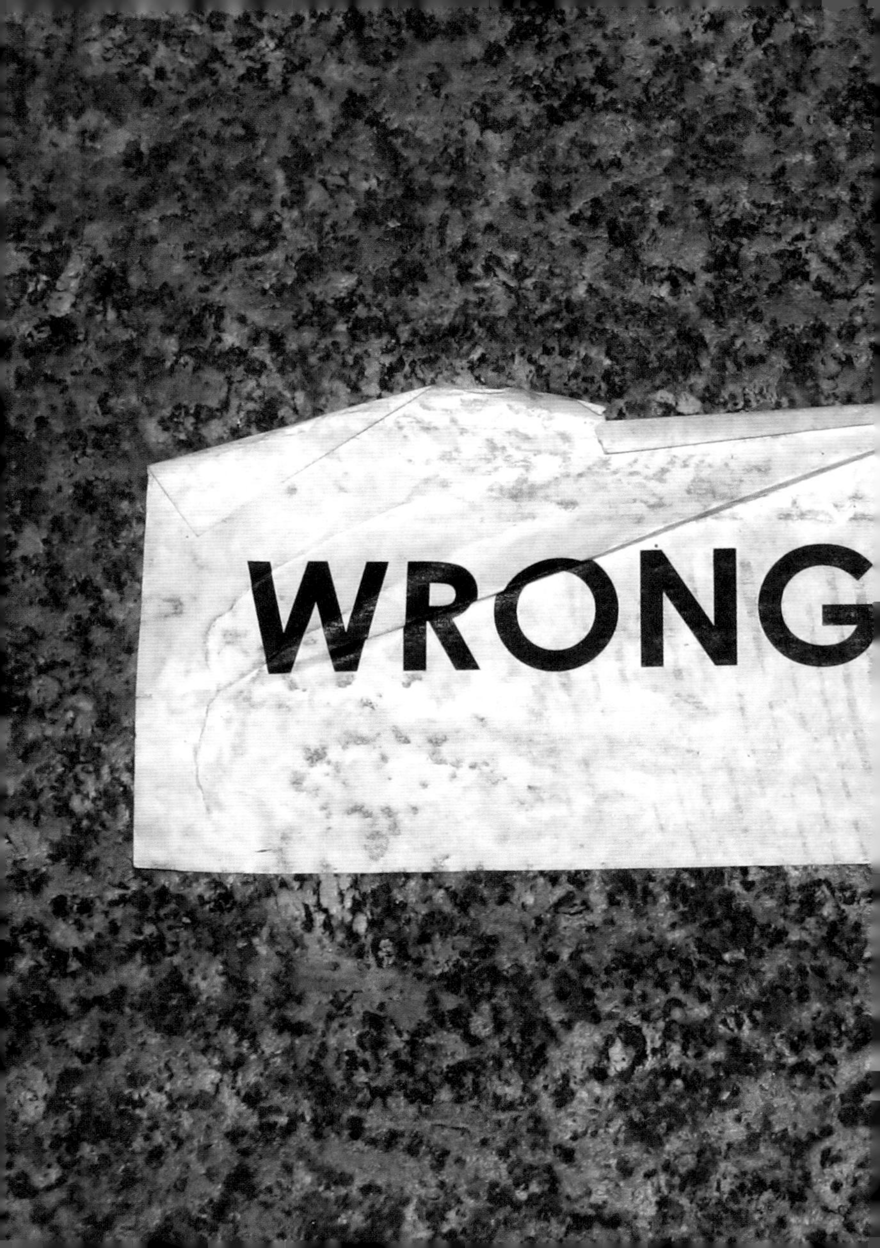

WRONG

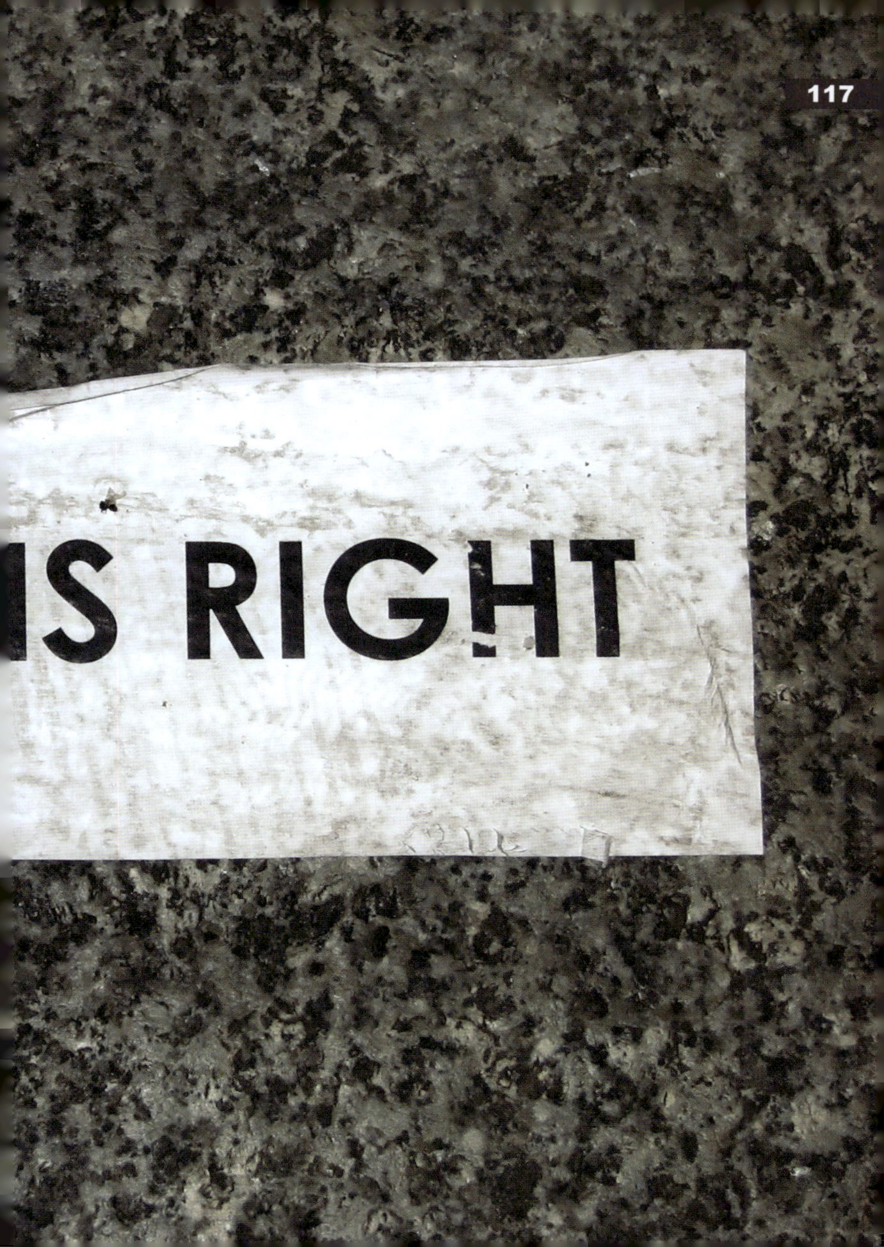

IS RIGHT

PLEASE YOURSELF

Forget about pleasing your client, editor or the paying public; according to American photographer Ralph Steiner (1899-1986) it's all about being and pleasing yourself: "Eventually I discovered for myself the utterly simple prescription for creativity; be intensely yourself. Don't try to be outstanding; don't try to be a success; don't try to do pictures for others to look at – just please yourself"

———————

"I'm trying to please myself; certainly that's a big criterion... though in a sense, I don't take images just for myself. I take images that I think other people will want to see. I don't take pictures to put in a box and hide them. I want as many people to see them as possible."
Mary Ellen Mark (1940), American photographer

"You have to fight for your work – everybody has to. You have to be able to get knocked down and stand back up. You can't let it stay on your shoulders. I see a lot of photographers who do their thing and put their soul in it and in the end it is all changed, but their name is still on it. So I do what Dick Avedon told me once and I just go out on each job and take pictures for myself. I'll photograph trees or if I meet a really handsome guy or girl I'll take their picture, even if they're not part of the set."
Bruce Weber (1946), American photographer

"I walked all around it [the Guggenheim Bilbao] and couldn't find one clear, clean shot. To make things worse, the weather was lousy. Nothing about this rang 'commercial money shot.' In a situation like this there's only one thing to do: forget about pleasing editors, please yourself."
Robert Polidori (1951), Canadian photographer

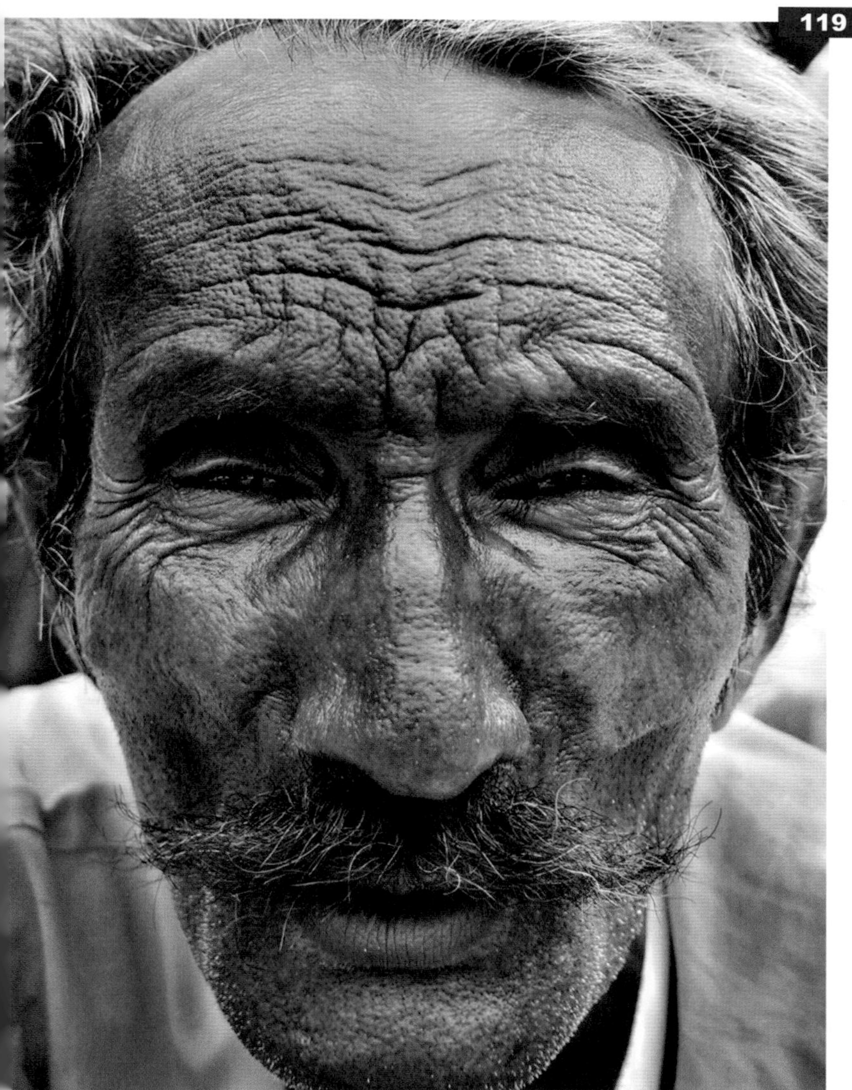

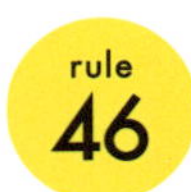

PHOTOGRAPHY IS A CALLING/ CAREER*

* delete as applicable

—————

"Young photographers should learn their craft well and not expect to make a constant living from taking pictures. But they should FOLLOW THEIR BLISS."
Dennis Stock (1928-2010), American photographer

"IT'S ABOUT TIME WE TAKE PHOTOGRAPHY SERIOUSLY, AND TREAT IT AS A HOBBY."

Elliott Erwitt (1928), French-born American photographer

"Photograph because you love doing it, because you absolutely have to do it, because the chief reward is going to be the process of doing it. Other rewards – recognition, financial remuneration – come to so few and are so fleeting. And even if you are somewhat successful, there will almost inevitably be stretches of time when you will be ignored, have little income, or – often – both. Certainly, there are many other easier ways to make a living in this society. Take photography on as a passion, not a career."
Alex Webb (1952), American photographer

"Forget about the profession of being a photographer. First be a photographer and maybe the profession will come after. Don't be in a rush to make pay your rent with your camera. Jimi Hendrix didn't decide on the career of professional musician before he learned to play guitar. No, he loved music and created something beautiful and that THEN became a profession. Larry Towell, for instance, was not a 'professional' photographer until he was already a 'famous' photographer. Make the pictures you feel compelled to make and perhaps that will lead to a career. But if you try to make the career first, you will just make shitty pictures that you don't care about."
Christopher Anderson (1970), Canadian photographer

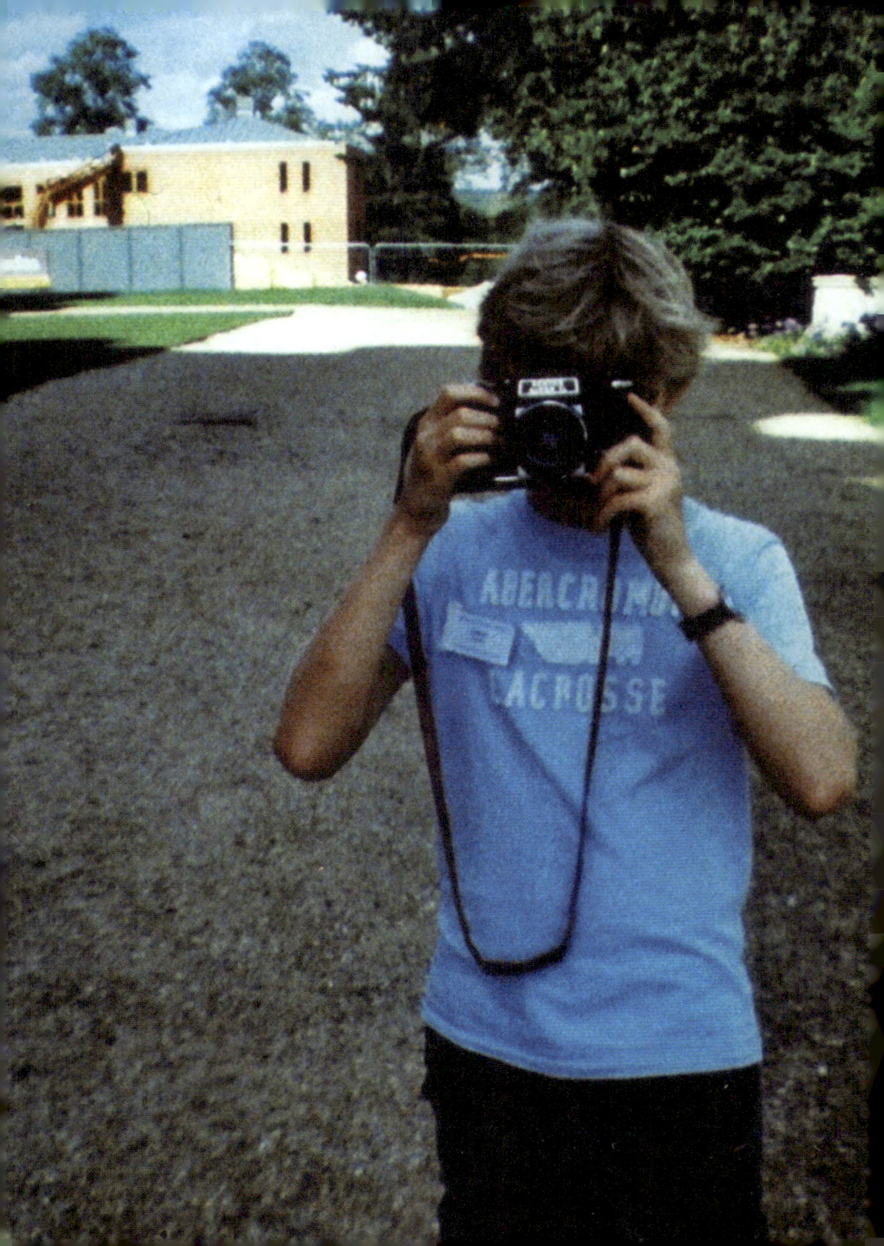

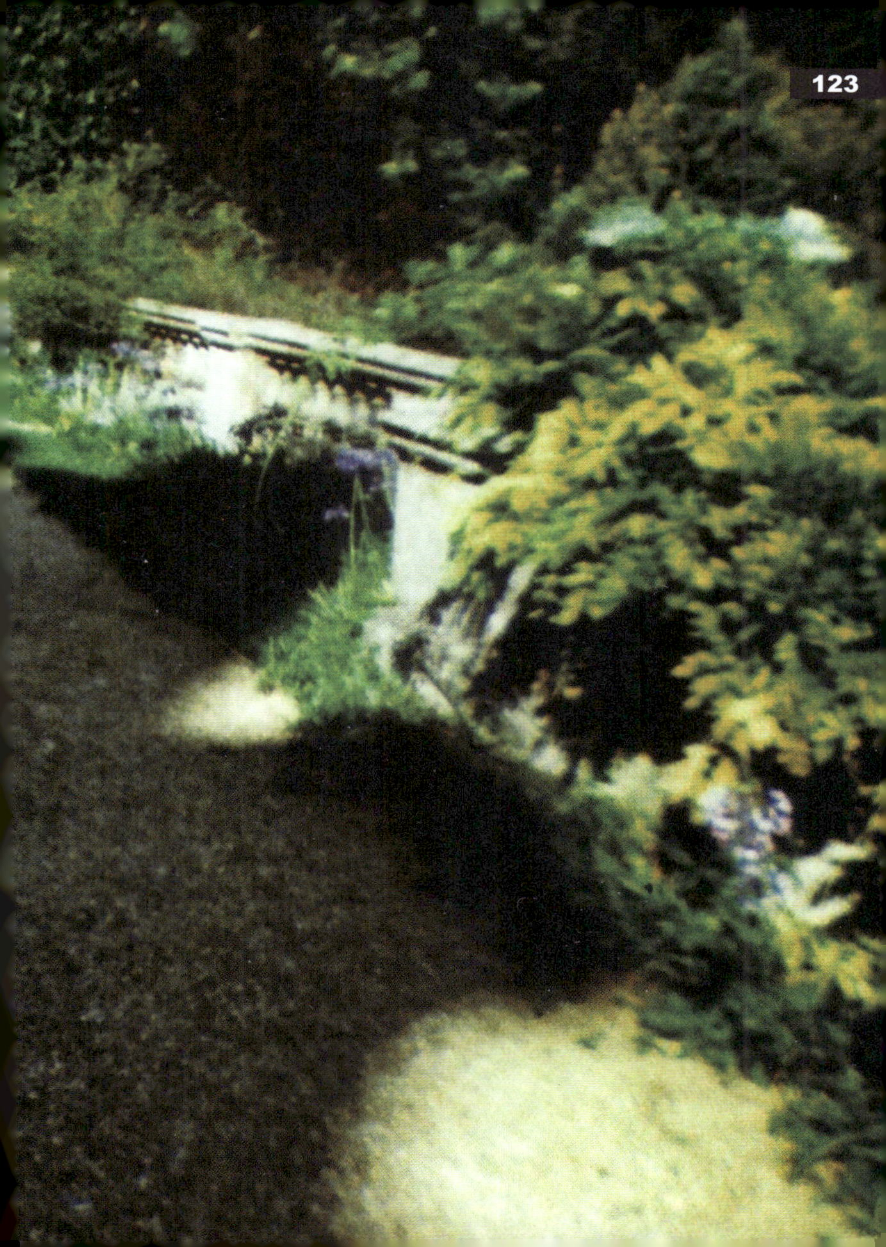

Nude photography is a form of art

The naked body has long been a welcome source of artistic inspiration. For centuries nudes inspired painters and sculptors alike. When photography came along, photographers were only too happy to continue the tradition.

———

"It was not until 1980 that I photographed what I consider to be my first nude. In quick succession I executed the Big Nudes, the Naked and Dressed, and, in Los Angeles, the Domestic Nudes series. The fact that the models in these photographs were the same girls I used in my fashion work gave them a certain elegance and coolness that I was looking for in my work."
Helmut Newton (1920-2004),
German-Australian photographer

"I am incredibly suspicious of photographers who specialize in the nude. I feel sure the majority takes these photographs because they want to see a girl without her clothes... Only very, very occasionally I see a picture of the nude that seemed to be worthwhile shooting purely for 'artistic' reasons…"
David Hurn (1934), British
photographer

"The female nude has been a rich and rewarding subject for photography since the medium was born. Photographs have approached this subject from every conceivable motive and every, infinitely complex, set of desires. Many, it is true, have been ugly, base and destructive. Some, however, have been exquisitely beautiful and elevating. The vast majority have been somewhere in between. Just like everything else in life."
Bill Jay (1940-2008), British
photographer and author

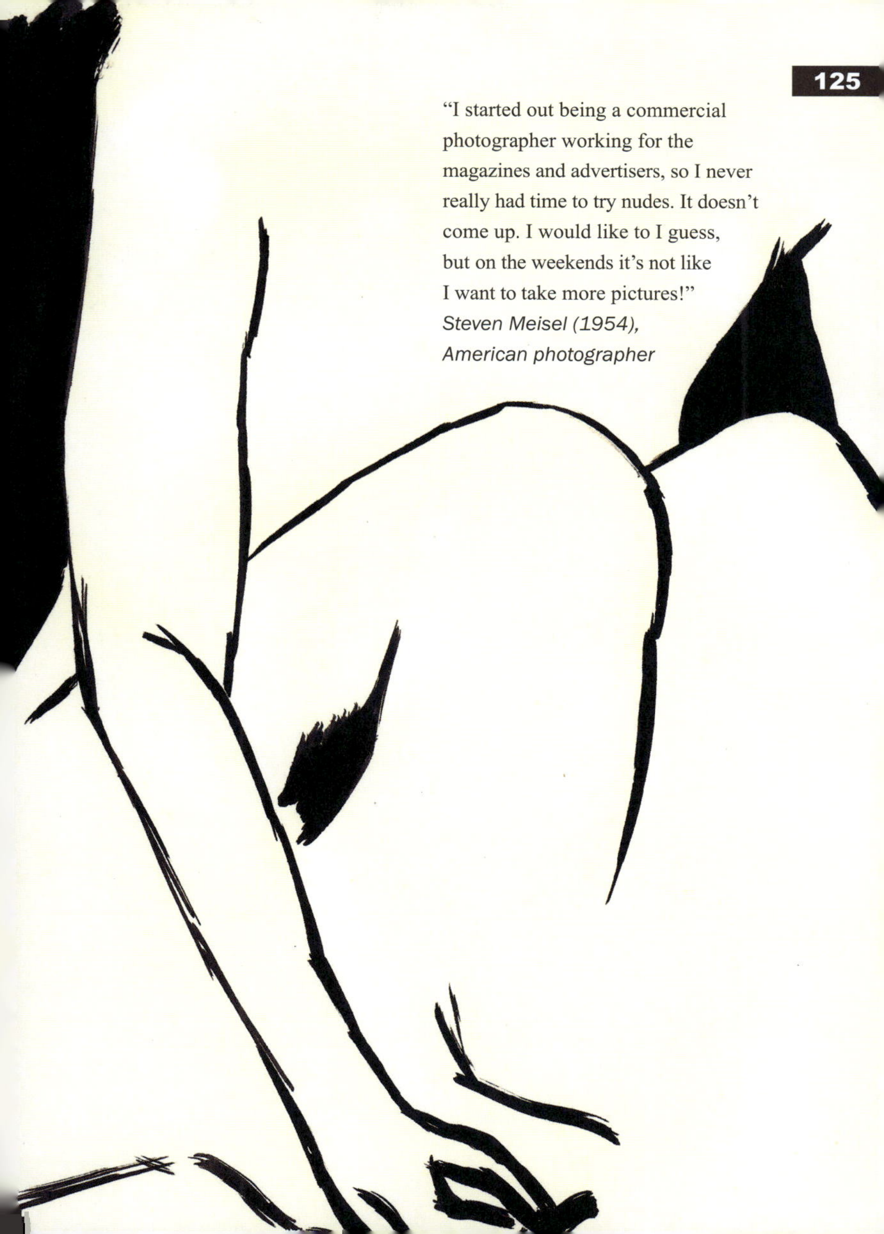

"I started out being a commercial
photographer working for the
magazines and advertisers, so I never
really had time to try nudes. It doesn't
come up. I would like to I guess,
but on the weekends it's not like
I want to take more pictures!"
Steven Meisel (1954),
American photographer

TAKE IT TO THE STREETS

The popularity of fashion blogs has resulted in renewed interest in street-style photography. The keyword here is renewed, because while The Sartorialist's Scott Schuman has often been hailed as the inventor of the genre, photographers have been taking to the streets since the late 19th century.

"People [have] been photographing the street since the camera was invented. At the turn of the 20th century, the horse races were the big thing. Lartigue was just a boy then. But the Séeberger brothers in France were taking pictures. They, and others, were commissioned by lace and fabric houses to go to the grand prix days at the Longchamp, Chantilly, Auteuil and Deauville racetracks and photograph fashionable women. The resulting albums were used as sample books by dressmakers."
Bill Cunningham (1929), American photographer

"When I ask to photograph someone, it is because I love the way they look and I think I make that clear. I'm paying them a tremendous compliment. What I'm saying is, I want to take you home with me and look at you for the rest of my life."
Amy Arbus (1954), American photographer

"There's a moment where you live vicariously, and are transported into the quiet life of a well-dressed man. The picture's not about fashion, it's about style, and how a unique individual lives his life in the world he creates for himself."
Scott Schuman (1968), American blogger and photographer

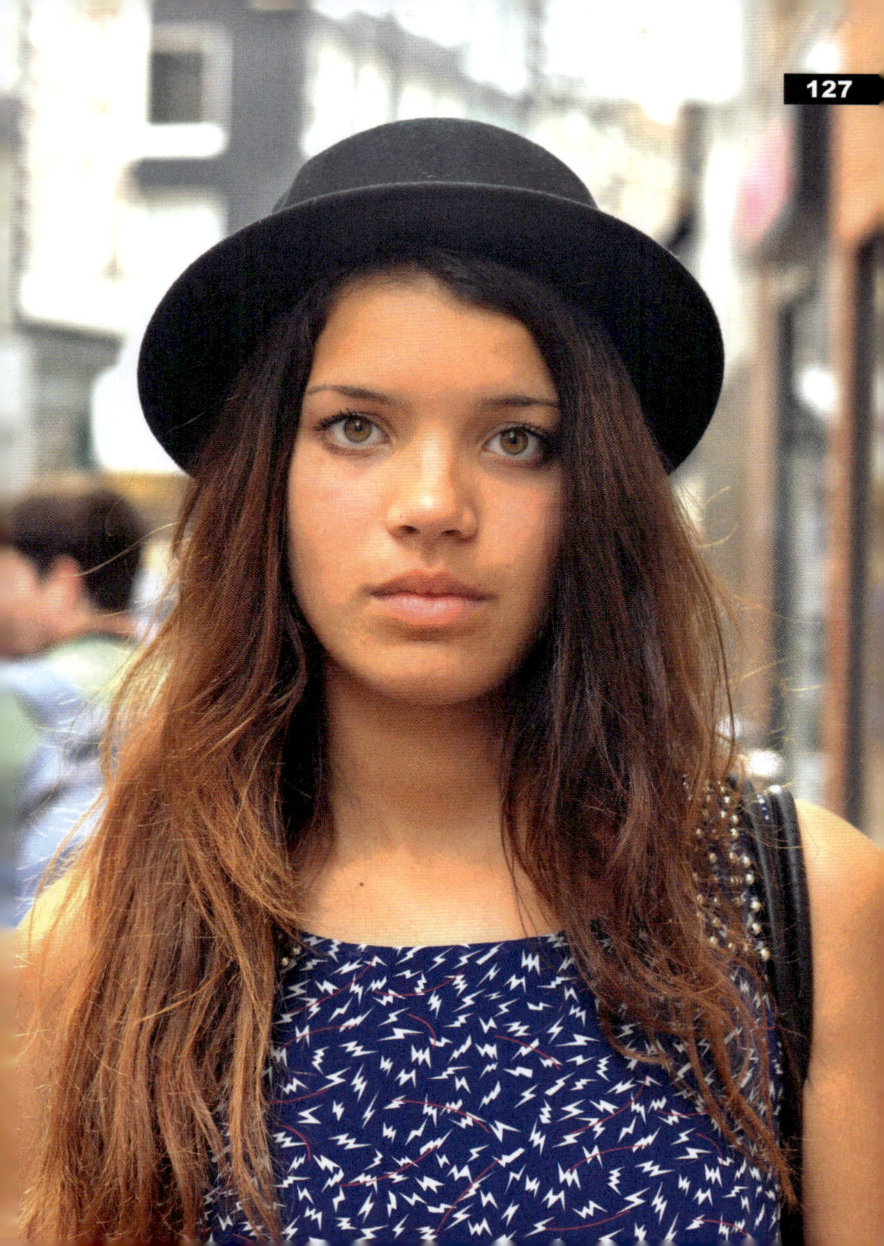

“*All photo*

memento m

Although we'd love to take credit for this adage, it actually comes from American writer and filmmaker Susan Sontag (1933-2004), who convincingly argued that "to take a photograph is to participate in another person's (or thing's) mortality, vulnerability, mutability."

———————

"It is no accident that the portrait was the focal point of early photography. The cult of remembrance of loved ones, absent or dead, offers a last refuge for the cult value of the picture. For the last time the aura emanates from the early photographs in the fleeting expression of a human face. This is what constitutes their melancholy, incomparable beauty."
Walter Benjamin (1892-1940),
German philosopher and critic

...raphs are ...ori."

"As time passes by and you look at portraits, the people come back to you like a silent echo. A photograph is a vestige of a face, a face in transit. Photography has something to do with death. It's a trace."
Henri Cartier-Bresson (1908-2004), French photographer

"I used to think that I could never lose anyone if I photographed them enough. In fact, my pictures show me how much I have lost."
Nan Goldin (1953), American photographer

TRY TO BE AS INVISIBLE AS POSSIBLE

For photojournalists, as well as street and documentary photographers it's of the utmost importance to be as invisible as possible. Their job is to report on, rather than intrude, or even worse, influence a particular scene. But as invisible as a photographer might make him or herself either on set or on location, in the end the final product – that is the photograph – always shows the maker. After all, as American photographer Mary Ellen Mark (1940) famously remarked, as a photographer you "reveal yourself by what you choose to photograph." So much for being invisible.

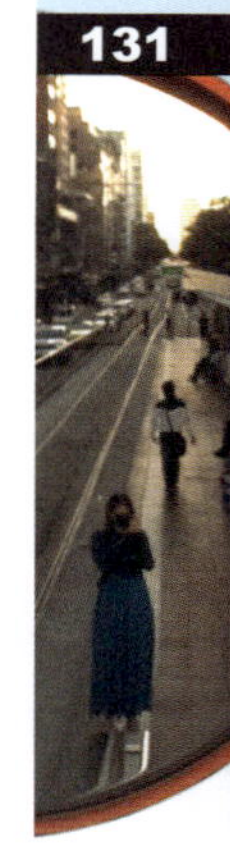

"All photographs are self portraits."
Minor White (1908-1976), American photographer

"My portraits are more about me than they are about the people I photograph."
Richard Avedon (1923-2004), American photographer

"I try to work as the invisible man and not be part of the story I am documenting. Let those you are photographing do their jobs and find the pictures in what they are doing without interfering with set-ups and posing."
Ted Grant (1929), Canadian photographer

"It (photography) has to be done discreetly and quietly. Invisible is the word."
Bill Cunningham (1929), American photographer

"I think you reveal yourself by what you choose to photograph, but I prefer photographs that tell more about the subject. There's nothing much interesting to tell about me; what's interesting is the person I'm photographing, and that's what I try to show."
Mary Ellen Mark (1940), American photographer

"You are a big part of your picture. Even when you are trying to blend in and be invisible on the scene, you are still behind that lens."
Rena Effendi (1977), Azerbaijani photographer

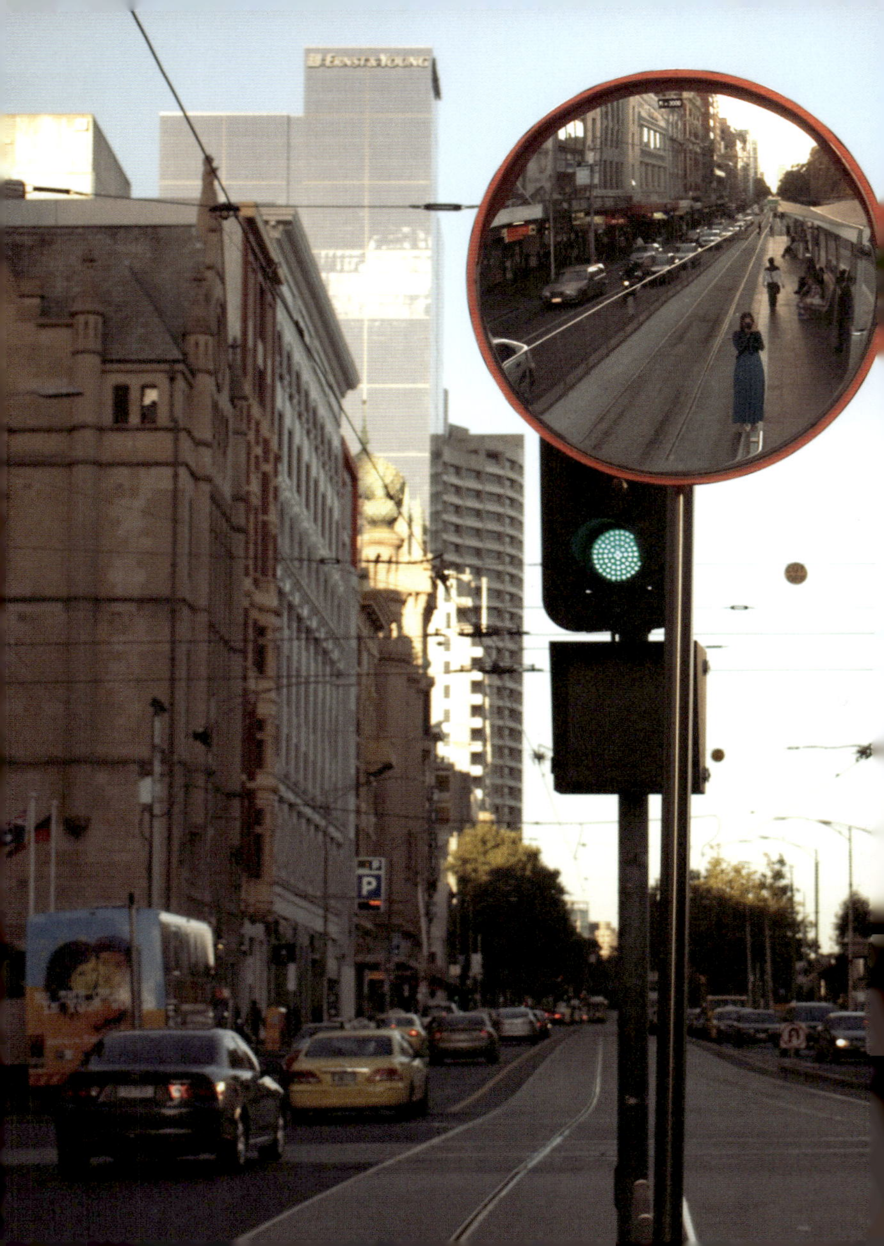
Ernst & Young

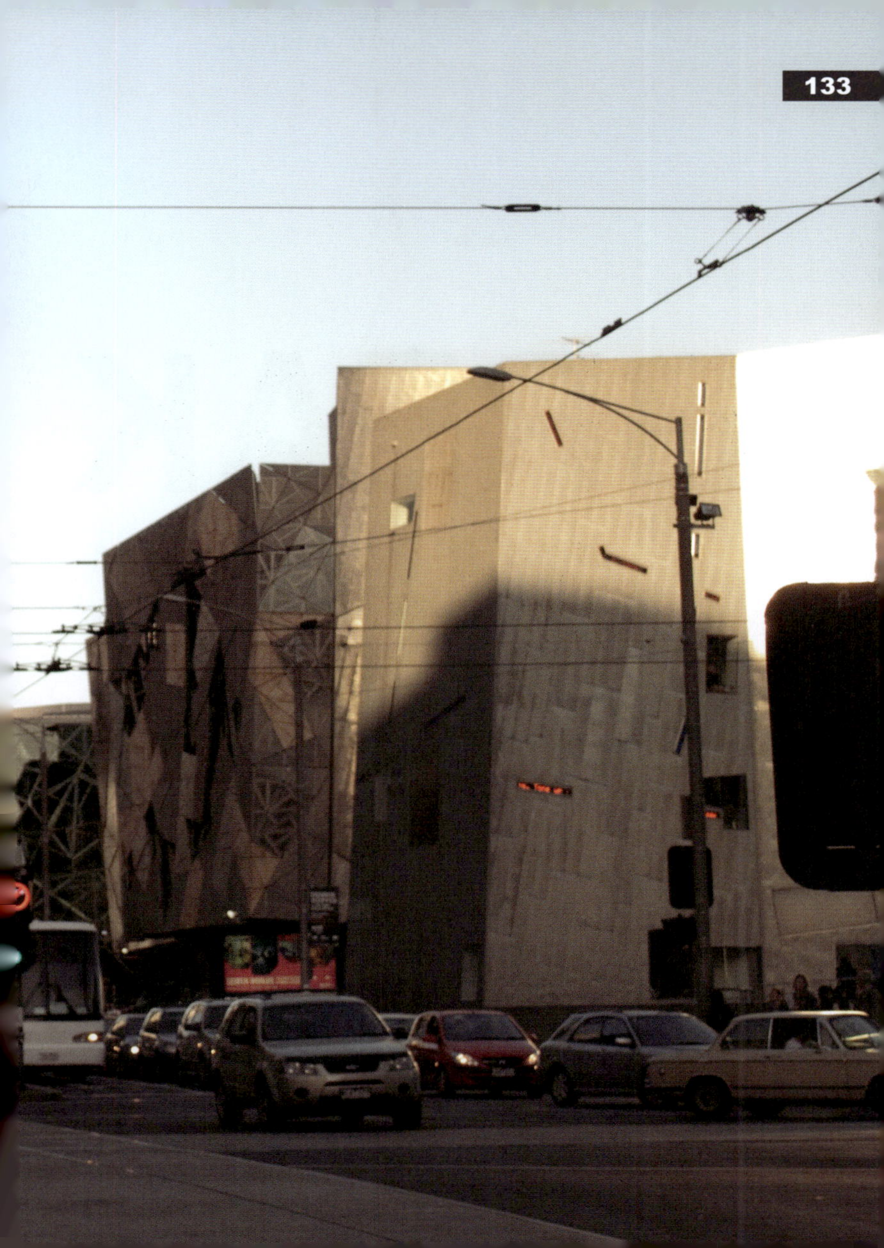

BREAK THE RULES

Now you know all the rules and have read the opinions of photographers the world over, it's high time to break the rules and form your own opinion and photographic vision.

———————

"There are no rules for good photographs, there are only good photographs."
Ansel Adams (1902-1984),
American photographer

"Photography is not a sport. It has no rules. Everything must be dared and tried!"
Bill Brandt (1904-1983), British
photographer

"I'm not aware of rules. I'm sure they're there, based on virtue of sensibility. I think sensibility imposes an organizing principle, a structure for how you work, but I don't think I carry with me a set of... I guess rules is a pretty strict way of looking at it."
Larry Sultan (1946-2009),
American photographer

"Respect and work within photography's limitations, you will go much further."
Donovan Wylie (1971), British
photographer

CONTRIBUTORS

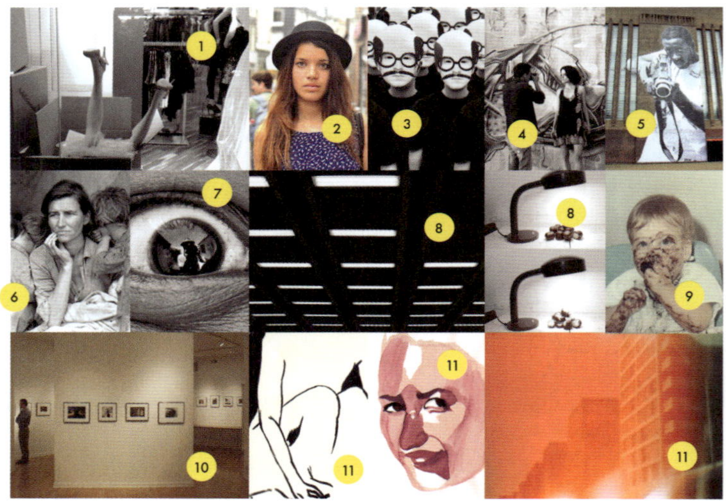

1 Keoni Cabral (cc)
(http://www.flickr.com/keoni101)
2 Barbara Iweins
(www.aucoindemarue.wordpress.com)
3 Phil Hearing (cc)
(http://www.philhearing.com)
4 abbilder (cc)
(http://www.flickr.com/abbilder)
5 Jim Linwood (cc)
(www.flickr.com/brighton)
6 Dorothea Lange

7 JR
(http://www.jr-art.net)
8 Wink & Shoot / Lianne van de Laar
(www.winkandshoot.com)
9 Howdy, I'm H. Michael Karshis (cc)
(www.flickr.com/hmk)
10 dbking (cc)
(www.flickr.com/bootbearwdc)
11 Lilian van Dongen Torman
(www.lilianvandongentorman.com)

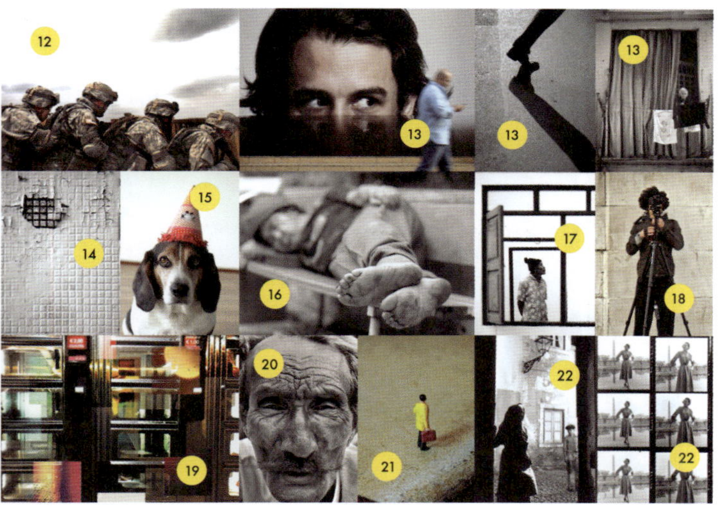

12 The U.S. Army 🅒🅒
(www.flickr.com/soldiersmediacenter)
13 Thomas Leuthard 🅒🅒
(www.flickr.com/thomasleuthard)
14 hobvias sudoneighm 🅒🅒
(www.flickr.com/striatic)
15 Sarah B. 🅒🅒
(www.flickr.com/prettyinprint)
16 Jim Fischer 🅒🅒
(www.flickr.com/jimfischer)
17 Björn Bechstein 🅒🅒
(www.flickr.com/bechstein)

18 Garry Knight 🅒🅒
(www.flickr.com/garryknight)
19 Janne Ettwig
(www.stilbruch.nl)
20 anurag agnihotri 🅒🅒
(www.flickr.com/agnihot)
21 JD Hancock 🅒🅒
(www.flickr.com/jdhancock)
22 Toni Frissell

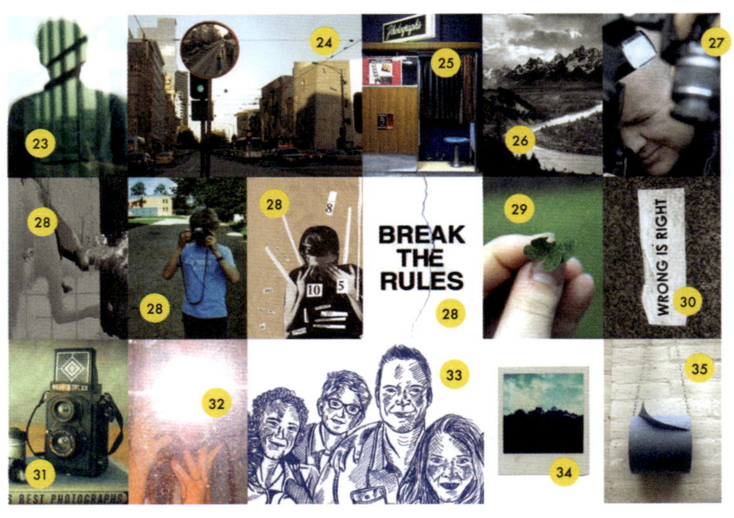

BREAK
THE
RULES
WRONG IS RIGHT
'S BEST PHOTOGRAPHS

Thanks to:
Premsela, Dutch Platform for Design and Fashion (www.premsela.org)
Lemon scented tea (www.lemonscentedtea.com)

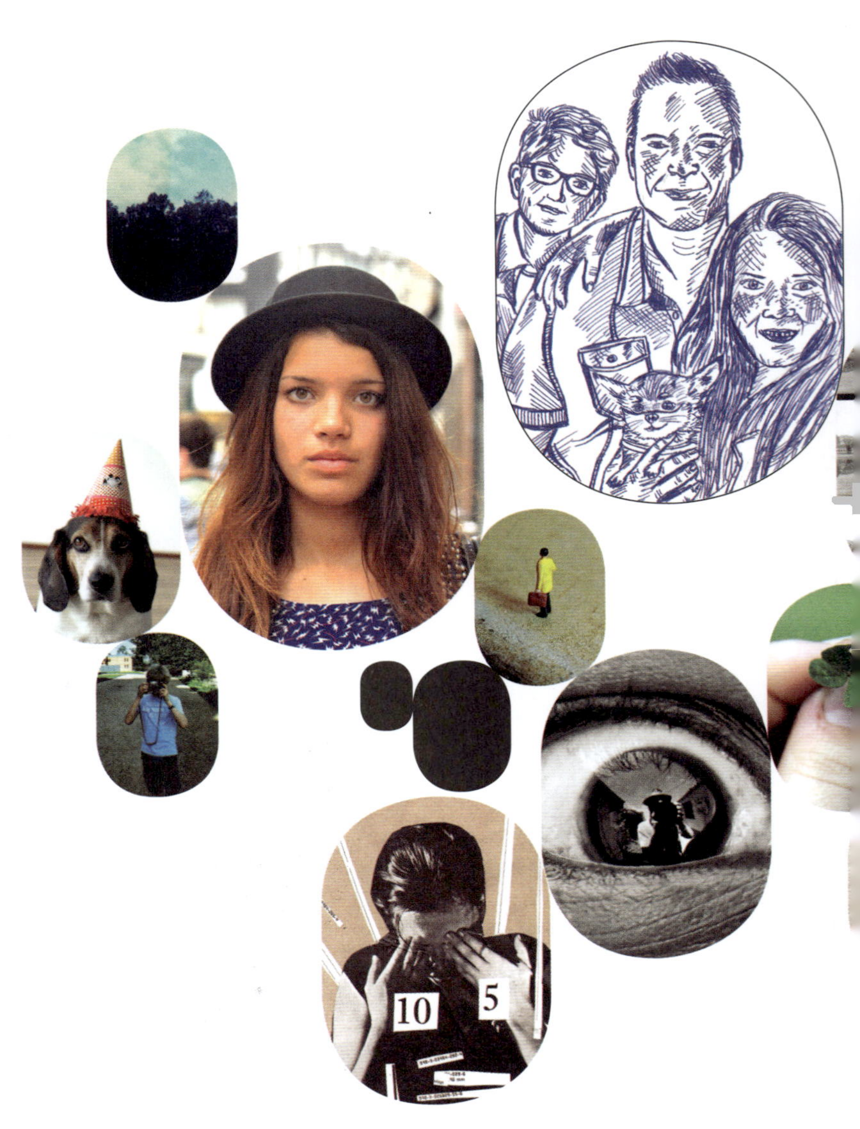